R.A.P. Therapy For Your Prosperity

Learn SELF-EMPOWERMENT for Positive Change

by

KEITH E. JACKSON, M.A.

1663 LIBERTY DRIVE, SUITE 200
BLOOMINGTON, INDIANA 47403
(800) 839-8640
WWW.AUTHORHOUSE.COM

First published by AuthorHouse 10/12/05

ISBN:1-4208-3992-6 (sc)

Printed in the United States of America
Bloomington, Indiana

This book is printed on acid-free paper.

TABLE OF CONTENTS

DEDICATION

This book is dedicated to my mom and dad that taught me I could do anything that I put my mind to. I also would like to include my two children Jared and Cassandra, you are living examples that R.A.P. works.

ACKNOWLEDGEMENTS

I would first like to thank Jehovah Jireh for His assistance and faithfulness. I know that I can always count on You to provide for all my needs. I want to thank my family for all their support and patience throughout the years. I also need to thank Carlene and David for the use of your time and talents on this project. In addition, I would like to acknowledge all my professors and fellow classmates at Southern California Bible College & Seminary. Thanks for sharing your knowledge and lives with me. I would also like to express my gratitude to The San Diego County Sheriff's Department for allowing me the opportunity and freedom to assist inmates in making positive choices for their lives. Finally, I like to thank all the people I have the pleasure to come into contact with. Thanks for your trust and sharing your life experiences with me. I pray that God smile upon you always.

PART I

RESPONSIBILITY

One day I was asked to teach a drug education class at one of the local detention facilities. The regular teacher was out on vacation, and rather than canceling the class I agreed to cover for the teacher. As was the regular custom the inmates came into the classroom, briefly congregated around the coffee pot, poured themselves a cup or two, and then found a seat. I immediately started the meeting by asking, "How many of you think that you are in here because of your substance abuse problem?" Almost every hand shot up in the air. I then asked the group how many people do you think have substance abuse problems in the United States? Nobody could answer the question; so I told them that according to a recent report, it has been estimated that approximately 54 million people have documented

3

substance abuse problems. I then asked how many people do you think are incarcerated in this country? I immediately informed them that the number is approximately 2.1 million. (Rose, Pens, Wright, 1998)

I concluded this portion of the session by reporting to them that according to USA Prison records, that it has been estimated that approximately 57% of those incarcerated have drug related charges (Rose, Pens, Wright, 1998), which means that out of the 2.1 million people incarcerated in our penal system, approximately 1.197 million are in there because of drugs. "If this is true, all of you that think you are in here only because of your substance problems have been misled. The reason being is that it has been reported that approximately 54 million people in the United States have substance abuse issues. With that figure in mind, there should be 54 million people incarcerated instead of 2.1 million."

Brief silence fell on the room, as the inmates took a minute to digest the information just given to them. No one could argue against the logic of the statement that I made. The crutch that many of them had held to so tightly had been kicked out from under them.

One inmate in the back on the room defiantly stated, "Well that might be true, but I have a disease". (He was referring to the term for those that are plagued with substance abuse addiction). I then asked this inmate if he knew the etiology of the term "disease" in the context of substance abuse, because I felt that he did

4

not totally understand. He proudly stated that he had been going to Alcohol Anonymous meeting for several years, and they often refer that those who are addicted to alcohol suffer from a disease. I then told him that this is only partially true.

I think that many times a half-truth can be just as damaging as a whole lie. There are many people running around blaming their relapses on this faulty assumption that some disease over which they have no control plagues them.

At this point I explained to the class what is meant when someone refers to "disease" in reference to alcoholism and substance abuse. Dorland's Medical Dictionary 1965 defines disease as, "A definite morbid process having a characteristic train of symptoms; it may affect the whole body or any of its parts, and its etiology, pathology, and prognosis may be known or unknown." I further explained in the late 1940's, E.M. Jellinek began to study alcoholism in over a thousand members of Alcoholics Anonymous. He found that alcoholism had a characteristic set of signs and symptoms, and it had a definite progressive course. As a result, in 1956, The American Medical Association formally recognized alcoholism as a disease. Up until that time, medical science, and society in general, believed that someone who was chemically dependent was a person with either a moral problem or weak willed.

The term was never to be used as some people use the term, as if they have some debilitating disease that has no cure. It was not meant to be used as a reason to excuse someone from accepting responsibility for maintaining their sobriety.

Needless to say that inmate never attended another substance abuse class. You see, we have a choice to make when confronted with the truth. We can accept it and grow, or run away from it and remain in the confines of our self-deception.

The reason why I chose to confront this group's belief system was to expose them to the irresponsibility of their thought process in relation to their substance abuse issues. Basically, a majority of those in attendance saw themselves as victims of their addiction over which they had no control. The truth of the matter is yes, they did suffer from the disease of drug addiction, but it is self-induced. This means that if they made the choice to abstain from using, they could reverse the process of addiction. There are millions of former addicts that are living prosperous lives free from the grip of alcoholism and substance abuse because they choose to take responsibility for their actions and seek proper treatment for their addiction of choice. So if one person is able to overcome their affliction of substance abuse, so can anyone who chooses to assume the responsibility for their actions.

The point of all this is to demonstrate the importance of inculcating the principle of responsibility into your thought processes. With it comes the empowerment needed to make positive change. We now need to come to an understanding of what the word "responsibility" means in the context of this book.

RESPONSIBILITY, WHAT DOES IT MEAN?

If an individual is to live up to their potential in this society, there are two things they need to understand. First, each human being is created as a free moral agent, which simple means that they have the freedom to make choices. Secondly, each human being has the power of self-direction. If both of these statements are true, then it can be said that each mature individual is responsible for his or her actions and behavior. According to Dr. Viktor Frankl, "Man is ultimately self-determining. Man does not simply exist but always decides what his existence will become in the next moment". (Frankl 1984)

Before we go any further, it would be prudent to define what is meant when I use the word "responsibility" in the context of this book. When I use the word "responsibility", I want you to think, "Being in charge". In other words, to be responsible means to be in control. Now, let's take this one step further. There are four things that each mature individual is responsible for: their thoughts, decisions, words, and actions.

If someone borrowed your car and returned it back to you damaged and made no provisions to compensate you for the damage they caused while using your vehicle, what would be the likelihood you would loan them your vehicle again? If you were like most people you would probably say, "Not likely." The main reason for the reluctance would be due to the irresponsible conduct of the person that borrowed your car. Because the person acted irresponsibly with your possession, they lost the privilege of using your vehicle.

In the same manner, in this country, which prides itself on freedom, it is important to understand that freedom has a price. That price is responsibility. If one does not exercise their responsibility, they are putting their freedom at risk. Think about those who are incarcerated for breaking criminal laws. Why have they lost the freedom experienced by those that are law abiding? Is it because they were not responsible for following the laws of society? Think about the privilege of using a credit card, buying a car, or buying a home. If an individual is responsible in paying their bills in a timely manner, banking institutions will be more likely to extend more credit to them. Conversely, if they are not responsible in paying their bills on time, they will either lose the privilege of borrowing money, or borrow at a higher interest rate.

The bottom line is that we cannot exist in an orderly free society without being responsible. As Frankl stated, "Freedom is in danger of degenerating into mere arbitrariness unless it is lived in terms of responsibleness". (Frankl, 1984 p. 134) There is a price to enjoying freedom, and that is being responsible.

RESPONSIBILITY AND CONSEQUENCES

One of the major characteristics of being responsible is accepting the consequences of your choices. Many people will readily deflect any responsibility for their actions by blaming others. This practice is a common defense mechanism used to absolve one for taking responsibility for their misfortune; however, there is a price that is paid for this type of thinking.

Part of the growing process is making mistakes. However, if we refuse to accept responsibility for the poor choices we have made, we place ourselves in a position where growth cannot occur. This in turn leaves us in a state of arrested development. This is one explanation why many individuals that inhabit our penal institutions continue to return once they are released. Most of these individuals refuse to understand the concept of taking responsibility for their actions. Furthermore, they fail to understand the correlation between their choices and the consequences associated with their choices. Some of the consequences for being irresponsible are the following:

- **Loss of personal freedom.**
- **Loss of personal privileges.**

- **A decrease in self-esteem.**

- **Loss of trust by others.**

- **Loss of respect by others.**

- **Hardship to love ones.**

- **Possible social isolation.**

- **Possible social disfranchisement.**

- **Possible shortened life span.**

It would be foolish for a farmer to plant wheat during the planting season and get upset during the harvest because he did not reap corn. Well, that is how foolish some people are when they get upset because they begin to receive the consequences on their prior choices. Like it is stated in the scriptures, "Do not be deceived, God is not mocked; for whatever a man sows, this he will reap." (Gal 6:7 NIV) If we are responsible for our thoughts, and the decisions that result from those thoughts, then we are responsible for the consequences associated with those decisions. If you can remember this, you can begin to empower yourself for the future. So, begin to take charge of your life by becoming a more responsible person.

In summary, we must realize the potential that resides within each of us. In order to harness this potential, we need to understand the importance of accepting responsibility for the choices that we make in life. We must accept that blaming others for our problems may be ego soothing, but this mentality will ultimately stifle our personal growth. With an increase in personal responsibility comes a higher sense of empowerment because there is the realization that our personal choices control our future.

ACCOUNTABILITY

One day I was sitting in my office when I received a call from one of the housing modules in the jail. The deputy assigned to the module asked if I could come down to speak with one of the inmates. This inmate was visibly upset and was in need of some crisis intervention. I went down and met with the inmate. When I asked him what the problem was, he began to tell me that he just returned from court and was informed that he would not be released from custody.

The inmate began to report how devastating this was to his family. He told me that his wife could not afford to pay the rent and recently received an eviction notice. She also told him that she was having problems with their oldest child, and she needed him at home. As the inmate continued to talk about the impact that his incarceration was having on his family he began to get more upset. He then started to blame the judge for not being more sensitive to his personal needs. Then he blamed his attorney for not speaking up for him. Next, he blamed the district attorney and his probation officer for singling him out and not providing help for him. The distraught inmate finally stated, "They don't give a f_ _ k about me or my family!" In selfish indignation the inmate protested that his rights had been violated, and he wanted to file an appeal, and have his attorney fired.

After he finished his tirade, I reflected back what he had said. "So you are upset because you thought you should have been released. And you feel that the judge and your probation officer are out to get you. Furthermore, the reason you wanted to be released is because your family is suffering from your absence in the home." The inmate agreed with all my statements. I then asked him why he was arrested. It turned out that the inmate was arrested for violating his conditions of probation for not reporting to his probation officer and testing dirty on a urine test. I later learned that this was his third probation violation.

I then asked him, "Did you realize the possible consequences that could occur prior to your arrest?" The inmate stated that he did, but added he was not thinking about that at the time! I then asked him, "If you would have thought about the impact that your decisions would have on your family, would you have done what you did?" He replied, "Hell no, I love my family!" I then asked him, "What do you need to do the next time you are faced with this situation?" After several moments of silence the inmate said, "Think about my family?" I responded, "That is right." Even though the inmate was unable to change the court's decision, and his family continued to suffer from his absence, he learned the importance of being accountable to others.

Many people confuse responsibility with accountability. Though these two terms are closely related, there are differences between the two. We will discuss some of the differences in this chapter, and demonstrate why it is important to incorporate this concept into our thought process.

If you were to look up the word "accountable" in the dictionary you would find words such as, "to reckon, to render a reason, and to explain." So, based on these definitions, we can say that to be accountable means to be able to give an explanation for one's actions. As we have already learned, each mature individual is responsible for his or her actions. If this is true, it can be argued that the act of being accountable is being able to give an account for one's actions.

You might be asking yourself, "How can this information help me control myself?" Let me relate a story that happened at work one day. An inmate sent a request to my office wanting to talk. From the tone of the request, it sounded like it was an urgent matter. When I met with her, she was distraught because she did not know where her children were. She had been arrested in the presence of her children and there was no other adult at her residence at the time of her arrest. She cried and said that she just wanted to know where her kids were.

It was obvious to me that this woman was concerned about her children, so I allowed her to make a phone call to Child Protective Services. However, before I handed her the phone I asked her, "If you had of thought about your kids, would you have placed yourself in this position?" She looked at me and said, "No." I then told her to remember that the next time she was tempted to do something that would jeopardize her freedom and the well-being of her children.

It is my belief that if this woman had took the time to think about the impact that her behavior was going to have on her family, she would not have placed herself in a position of being arrested. This is why the principle of accountability is so important. The sense of accountability causes a person to consider others before making choices. Accountability connects us with others because we realize that our behavior impacts those around us. When we say someone is selfish, we are stating that this person takes little or no regard for the feelings and concerns of others.

ACCOUNTABILITY AND EMPATHY

Being accountable gives us the ability to empathize with others. To have empathy means you are able to put yourself in another person's position. In other words, you would not do anything to anyone that you did not want done to you. This is because you know what it feels like. Those that lack this ability to empathize are a danger to society because they lack the ability to connect with others. These types of individuals will lie, cheat, and steal, with little or no conscience about what they are doing to others. These individuals are often referred to as having anti-social or psychopathic personality.

ACCOUNTABILITY & YOUR HIGHER POWER

As human beings we have been given the ability to direct the course of our lives. This means that we are free moral agents, with the ability to make choices. However, with this ability comes accountability for we will have to give an account for the choices we have made to someone. Depending on your eschatology you may believe that you will ultimately have to give an account to God for what you have or have not done while on this earth. With this in mind, it is vital to understand the importance of having a sense of accountability to someone or something.

For example, those who are actively involved in Alcoholic Anonymous understand the importance of the principle of accountability in maintaining their sobriety. By being accountable to their sponsor and the other members of their respective group the individual can use the sense of accountability in fighting the temptation to take a drink.

I have found in almost every case where a person has relapsed back into their addiction, it started when they discontinued going to their meetings and or treatment. This started the chain reaction that ultimately led to their relapse. One explanation is they did not have someone to whom they were accountable to. Without the sense of accountability they lacked the personal restraint to abstain from their drug of choice.

HOW CAN ACCOUNTABILITY HELP YOU?

In essence, I have found that having a sense of accountability has prevented me from acting on various temptations. If you are honest with yourself, you will agree that we all are tempted in numerous ways; however, if you ask those who are successful in overcoming their temptations regularly, you will find a common theme. It is the basic concept of being accountable to someone, or something. It could be God, family, employer/employees, friends, or the community. When tempted, these individuals probably think, "what would they think, or how would they feel if I did…"

With this sense of accountability you gain an additional weapon in your fight for self-control. The stronger the sense of accountability the less power temptation has over you. As I stated previously, those individuals that lack in the ability to empathize with others generally do not experience a connectedness with others. As a result, they have little or no sense of accountability to others. This frees them do whatever they see fit, with little or no regard for others.

ACCOUNTABILITY & MORAL DEVELOPMENT

The importance of morality in our society is indispensable. The founders of this nation understood that a self-governing nation is built upon self-governing individuals, and personal self-government is achieved only by adherence to moral and religious principles. This sentiment was echoed in an address made by John Adams, the second President of the United States to the military on October 11, 1798.

> **We have no government armed with power capable of contending with human passion unbridled by morality and religion...Our Constitution was made only for a moral and religious people. It is wholly inadequate to the government of any other. (America's God and Country Encyclopedia of Quotations, 1994)**

From my experience with the judicial system, I have found a correlation between those individuals with little or no sense of accountability versus those with a higher degree of accountability. When I was employed as a probation officer, I would make it a practice to inquire into the spiritual beliefs, familial, and community ties of those under my charge. Without fail those who had some sort of spiritual belief, as well as family and community ties were more successful on probation. One explanation could be they had a higher sense of moral development.

According to Lawrence Kohlberg, world-renowned psychologist and former professor at Harvard University, people progressed through different stages of moral development. His well-known theory of moral development was popularized in the 1970's through his research studies conducted at Harvard's Center for Moral Education. Kohlberg identified six identifiable stages of moral reasoning. (Kohlberg 1981) In this section I will discuss the first four stages.

Kohlberg identified the first stage of moral development as "Obedience and Punishment". This stage is generally found at the elementary school level and below, people behave according to socially acceptable norms because they are told to do so by some authority figure. This obedience is compelled by the threat or application of punishment.

At this stage the individual is unable or unwilling to internalize the abstract construct of right and wrong behavior. As a result, they become dependent on outside sources to make that determination for them. Therefore, right and wrong is based on the end results of a particular act. If an act results in an unpleasant consequence, the behavior is deemed wrong. This is how children begin to learn the difference between right and wrong behavior.

The second stage of moral development described by Kohlberg, is "Individualism, Instrumentalism and Exchange". Like the first stage of moral development right and wrong behavior is egocentric in nature. This stage of moral development is characterized by a view that right behavior means acting in one's best interest.

For example, a child receives a reward for their obedience to their parent or caregiver. What they have learned from this experience is that when I am obedient I get a reward, therefore this is right. Conversely, when I am disobedient I do not get a reward, therefore this is wrong.

According to Kohlberg, the third phase of moral development is called, "Good Boy/Girl". He observed that the individual moral focus shifts to an attitude which seeks to do what will gain the approval of others, such as parents, teachers, and friends.

At this point the individual seeks approval and conforms to someone else's expectations. When accused of doing something wrong, the excuse often given is "everyone is doing it" or "I did not intend to hurt anyone."

The fourth stage of moral development is referred to as "Law and Order." At this stage, one is generally oriented to abiding by the law and responding to the obligations of duty. There is an internalization of society's rules about how to behave. The individual generally feel an obligation to conform not only to the customs and values of their family and friends, but also to the laws and customs of society. It is interesting to note the emphasis placed on the sense of accountability to others, in Kohlberg's theory of moral development.

Many habitual criminals have the ability to disregard the feelings of others and society at large. They generally judge right and wrong with the probability of getting caught. In many cases when these individuals do get caught, the only remorse they have is because they got caught. This mentality is reflected in the first stage of Kohlberg's theory of moral development.

Just like all stages of development, an individual can experience arrested development at any particular stage. It is my belief that many habitual criminals function at a lower stage of moral development than the norm. However, with the higher sense of accountability to others this level of moral development can be elevated.

WHO ARE YOU ACCOUNTABLE TO?

When my children were young, I would make it a practice to go over the R.A.P. principles routinely while driving them to school. It was and is my belief that by doing this, I was inculcating into their consciousness the tools they would need to avoid the pitfalls that many of our young people fall into like: substance abuse, alcoholism, gangs, and promiscuity. Being that both my children are in their teens and not involved in any of the aforementioned, it's safe to say R.A.P. had something to do with it.

There are three basic areas that I focus on when teaching the concept of accountability to others. The three are spiritual, family, and community.

- **Spiritual. Having a sense of spiritual accountability is vital. I have found that spiritual values are intrinsic and universal. They are also absolute. It is my belief we were created in God's image and likeness. (Gen 1:26). God is Spirit. Therefore, a part of us is spirit, and that part of us eternal. With this understanding, one realizes that they will ultimately have to give an account for their life on this planet.**

- **Family. Having a sense of family accountability is important. Next to our relationship with God, there is no other more important relationship. The family is the catalyst of so-**

ciety. It is the family that instills the values that are reflected in our society. Any historian will tell you that prior to the downfall of any great nation, there was a breakdown of some kind within the family unit.

• **Community/fellowman.** Having a sense of accountability to others will assist us in sharing a connectedness with them. This connectedness will increase our ability to empathize with others and to consider the impact of our actions on them. It forces us to consider how our choices will affect others.

ACCOUNTABILITY AND RELATIONSHIPS

As previously stated, one of the aspects of being accountable is considering the thoughts and feelings of others. This sense of obligation to others fosters a sense of community because each individual is compelled to think outside of their personal self-interest, and begin to realize that they are not an identity unto themselves, but they are part of a community.

In conclusion, having a sense of accountability assists us in several areas. First, it causes us to use self-restraint because we have the capacity to think outside of our personal interests. This type of egocentric thinking can lead to a deviant and destructive lifestyle. Secondly, it increases our sense of obligation to others, which increases a stronger sense of connectedness with others. Finally, it also assists us in insulating ourselves from behaving in a self-serving manner.

I would like to close this section with an illustration from the Bible. One day Jesus was asked by one of the chief religious figures of this time, "What was the greatest commandment?" Jesus answered him by stating, "Love God with all your heart, soul, and mind. And love your neighbor as you love yourself." (Mark 12:28-34). So in essence, what Jesus said was to consider and be sensitive to God and your fellow man. If we follow this advice we will find life to be more satisfying.

"Duty is ours; results are God's."

In September, 1811, John Quincy Adams wrote a letter to his son from St. Petersburg, Russia, while serving for the second time as an ambassador to that country:

"It is in the Bible, you must learn them, and from the Bible how to practice them, those duties are to God, to your fellow-creatures, and to yourself."Thou shalt love the Lord thy God, with all thy heart, and with all thy soul, and with all thy mind, and with all thy strength, and thy neighbor as thy self." On these two

commandments, Jesus Christ expressly says, "Hang all the law and the prophets"; that is to say, the whole purpose of Divine Revelation is to inculcate them efficaciously upon the minds of men...

"Let us, then, search the Scriptures ... The Bible contains the revelation of the will of God. It contains the history of the creation of the world, and of mankind; and afterward the history of one peculiar nation, certainly the most extraordinary nation that has ever appeared upon the earth.

"It contains a system of religion, and of morality, which we May examine upon its own merits, independent of the sanction it receives from being the Word of God...

"(America's God and Country Encyclopedia of Quotations, 1994)

PURPOSE

Sam was a model inmate. He could hold a pleasant conversation, and he was intelligent. Overall, Sam was a likeable person. That was what was so puzzling about him. I used to think to myself, "Why does this guy continue to come back to jail?" According to his arrest record, Sam had an extensive criminal record dating back to his juvenile years.

I encouraged Sam to enroll in the RAP class. Sam finally came to the session that addressed the importance of having a sense of purpose. One of the first questions I asked was, "What are other words that we could use instead of 'purpose'?" Some of the answers were: "reason, goal", and "mission". I then went around and asked each person, "What is your reason for living?"

Everyone searched for an appropriate response. Some said, "To get out of jail." Others stated, "To make a lot of money." Some responded by saying, "To have a good time." A few admitted that they really did not have a purpose at all.

After the class ended Sam came up to me and said, "I know why I keep coming back here, I never really had a reason not to. I'm a good inmate; I know the system, and every time I come here, I am selected to be a trustee. That makes me feel special." He continued, "What I learned today is that I never really had a purpose to live. I did not have something to get excited about. That's why I do drugs and commit crime because it gives me something to get excited about." Sam concluded, "I know what I need to do; I'm going to write out some goals and find a purpose for my life."

Sam finally decided that he really enjoyed doing landscaping and auto detailing. He decided that he would take some courses at the local community college to help him to get started. He also connected with his uncle, who already had a landscaping business, to see if he could work for him upon his release. Sam started mapping out what he planned to do when he was released.

Prior to Sam's release, he was filled with excitement. He exclaimed, "I feel good about myself! I just spoke to my probation officer and shared my goals with him. He said that he would help me. Man, this stuff really works!" Upon his release Sam made it a point to stop by and thank me. To make a long story short, Sam is currently working, going to school to finish his Associates Arts degree, and attending church. In addition, he is due to be terminated from probation shortly. All Sam needed was to find a sense of purpose for his life! In this chapter we will look at the reasons why having a sense of purpose for your life is so important.

The final component of R.A.P. is purpose. Purpose serves as an integral principle of R.A.P. therapy. Without it, any effort put forth in the area of self-change will not last for any substantial period of time. There are many people who have good intentions to make positive changes in their lives, but only a few are able to achieve their goal. Why? The main reason is that most people lack a sense of urgency necessary to complete the task at hand. So, it is vitally important to understand the importance of incorporating a sense of purpose for your life.

THE NEED FOR PURPOSE

Think about a time when you decided to make a change in your life. At first, you felt good about the decision you made. It excited you. You were motivated and energized with your commitment to change. Then as time passed, the motivation slowly began to dissipate, and before long, you found yourself back in the same pattern of behavior that you swore to change.

From personal experience, I have found this occurs because the sense of motivation no longer exists. The vision of what I wanted to accomplish was lost. Without the vision, the energy necessary to maintain focus vanishes. It has been my observation that the more a person can generate a sense of purpose within themselves, the better able they are to maintain the sense of motivation necessary to complete their goals.

WHAT IS THE MEANING OF PURPOSE

If you look at the definition of purpose in the dictionary, you will find four words commonly associated with this word. These four words are: "reason, meaning, goal," and "mission." So, it can be easily argued that with a sense of purpose, an individual can acquire a sense of meaning for their life. This in turn will give a person a reason to live. If a person has a meaning and a reason to live, they are more inclined to find something fulfilling to do with their life.

Dr. Viktor Frankl stresses the importance of experiencing a sense of meaning for one's own life. Frankl speaks from his own personal experience of being a prisoner of war in a Nazi death camp. In his book, Man's Search for Meaning, Frankl speaks of the horrid conditions he endured in such places as Auschwitz. From this experience he developed the basic concepts of Logo Therapy. One of the statements that he made which had a profound impact on me was, "There is nothing in the world, and I venture to say, that would so effectively help one to survive even the worst conditions as the knowledge that there is a meaning in one's life." He continued, "There is much wisdom in the words of Nietzsche, 'He who has a why to live for can bear almost any how.'" (Frankl, 1984 p.109)

In my profession I encounter many individuals who felt that life has dealt them a bad hand. They are quick to recount all the injustices done to them as a viable explanation for their misbehavior. This type of mentality leads them to view themselves as being a victim of life. What I generally point out is that life is not fair. It never has been nor will be. The choice that we have to make is whether to dwell in the past or look to the future. Having a sense of purpose can provide us with a reason to live in spite of the circumstances we find ourselves in, no matter who or what is to blame.

There are three things to remember when establishing a sense of meaning for your life. First, you must believe that you have a task or mission to accomplish on this earth, and actively seek to fulfill that mission. The quickest way to build someone's self-esteem is having them do something they feel good about. It has been clinically demonstrated that when an individual fulfills certain drives, the brain will activate certain neurotransmitters to stimulate the reward center of the brain. With the release such neurotransmitters such as dopamine and adrenaline, the individual will experience a self induced euphoric feeling. Other substances such as methamphetamines, cocaine, and tobacco can mimic the same effect. That is why these substances are so addictive.

Second, a sense of meaning can be found in relationships with others. The more we are able to focus on the needs of others, the more actualized we become as human beings. This is the highest form of love that we can express to another human being, the giving of ourselves. The Bible states that God so loved the world that He gave his only Son. God expressed His love to mankind by the act of giving His Son. (John 3:16) There have been times in my life where I gave of myself when I would rather not; but every time that I did this, I was glad that I did. The sense of fulfillment that I experienced was well worth the temporary inconvenience.

Third, as I stated before, life is not fair. Bad things sometimes happen to "good" people for no apparent reason. It is just part of living on this planet. I heard it said it is not what happens to us that have the most impact, but it is our response that is the most important. We must strive to develop what Frankl calls a "tragic optimism". This is the ability of turning adversity into a platform to change ourselves for the better, deriving from life's instability an incentive to take responsible action.

Lastly, establishing a sense of purpose can provide for us a meaning for being. There are many individuals that turn to drugs and crime because they have a vacuum which they cannot fill. Many individuals destroy themselves because they realize that chasing after material gain has not provided them with the happiness that it promised. It is my contention that the happiest people in this world are not necessarily the richest, but they are those who have found a sense of meaning for their lives.

THE CONSEQUENCES OF MEANINGLESS

According to Frankl, what plagues most industrial societies today is the sense of meaninglessness. Many have pursued happiness and self-gratification to find self-fulfillment; however, it is the individual who finds a meaning for their life who finds lasting happiness. Another phenomenon that occurs with the sense of meaninglessness is the use of drugs. Frankl stated, "In fact the drug scene is one aspect of a more general mass phenomenon in our industrial societies."(Frankl, 1984 p.141) It was Frankl's contention that the feeling of meaninglessness plays an ever-increasing role in the etiology of many psychological disorders.

One of the most depressing books in the Bible to me is Ecclesiastes. However, there is a message in this book for the discerning reader. The writer of this book was Solomon, the son of King David. Solomon was the wisest and richest king of his time. Rulers and chief officials from all over the known world sought to have an audience with him. He ruled the Nation of Israel when it was at its zenith. During his reign, the nation experienced peace and great prosperity.

Yet with all this achievement, the first two chapters of Ecclesiastes he expounds on the meaninglessness of everything in life; he even included the seeking of wisdom and the pursuit of happiness. Of wisdom he wrote.

> *I thought to myself, Look, I have grown and increased in wisdom more than anyone who has ruled over Jerusalem before; I have experienced much of wisdom and knowledge. Then I applied myself to the understanding of wisdom, and also of madness and folly, but I learned that this too, is a chasing after the wind. (Ecc 1:16-17 NIV)*

What Solomon and Frankl realized is the importance of finding a reason for living, other than just for material gain and self gratification. That is not enough to guarantee us self-fulfillment. We must seek to find our eternal purpose of living to achieve this.

THE NEED FOR A VISION

Another important aspect of having a sense of purpose is it can provide the individual with a sense of direction.

Everyone gets distracted from time to time, but it is the person who has a strong sense of purpose who will be able to maintain their focus. One of the main reasons for this has to do with the individual's ability to visualize what they are trying to achieve.

Having a vision creates an image within a person's consciousness that strengthens their belief system. Many professionals in the field of psychology are beginning to understand the importance of the spiritual aspect of the human composition. In the past, it was generally accepted that spiritual belief had no place in modern psychology. In fact, Sigmund Freud looked down on religion and found it to be oppressive to the human condition. However, Frankl recognized the importance of having some sort of spiritual or religious belief. He stated, "When a patient stands on the firm ground of religious belief, there can be no objection to making use of the therapeutic effect of his religious convictions and thereby drawing upon his spiritual resources."(Frankl, 1984. p.122)

There are many people who live their lives with no sense of purpose. They generally live for the moment or vicariously through others. Why are reality shows are so popular? Why do people flock to stadiums and arenas to watch sporting events? One of the reasons is that people long to fill the vacuum that only a sense of purpose can fill. Some people live their entire lives only fulfilling their basic bodily needs, walking around like a donkey with a carrot dangling in front of its' face.

They live life merely existing from one day to the next. The bad part about this is that they do not even realize it. We need to have a vision which gives us focus and vitality. In the book of Proverbs it is stated that without a vision the people will perish (Prov 29:18a).

WAYS TO DEVELOP A SENSE OF PURPOSE

Hopefully by now, you should realize the importance of establishing a sense of purpose for your life. Some of you may even be asking yourself, "Where do I go from here?" There are several ways to develop a sense of purpose. Here are some of the ways that can assist you in this endeavor:

- **Seek spiritual enrichment. Get involved with an organization within the faith community with which you are affiliated.**

- **Become involved in your community in some capacity. Volunteer your time to some worthwhile organization of your choosing. Give of your talents and expertise to others.**

- **Take time to dream and visualize about what you would like to accomplish in the future. Get a vision for your life.**

- **Begin to pursue your dreams and visions.**

Purpose serves to provide us with a sense of meaning and gives us a reason for living. It also gives us direction. It provides us with energy and focus. It also gives us a reason to live and dream about the future. In essence, it gives us a reason for hope. Purpose enables us to persevere against the odds and to accomplish things once thought to be impossible. It causes us to endure hardships and find meaning and opportunity in the most adverse conditions. It causes us to look outside of ourselves and reach for a higher source of power. Without a sense of purpose, an individual will never know what it truly means to be alive.

In conclusion, I hope you realize the importance of establishing a sense of purpose for your life! Having a sense of purpose provides us with the ability to focus our attention to a specific goal or task. It also gives our life a sense of meaning or reason. With this sense of meaning, our lives can be energized with a new zest for living.

I would like to finish this chapter by recalling a situation that occurred several years ago. One day a friend of mine invited me to go out sailing with him. It was my first time going out in a sailboat. I never really wanted to go sailing because I thought it would be too much work. I would have rather gone out in a boat with an outboard motor because you do not have to depend on the wind. You just start the engine and go where you want to go.

Well, once we pulled away from the dock and cruised out of the bay, we started raising the sails. Once the sails were fully extended, I felt the thrust of wind surge us forward. It was quite a stimulating experience. I remember watching the waves colliding with the bow of the boat as we gained speed; then all of a sudden, we slowed down due the wind changing direction. My friend Mike then explained that we needed to change the position of the front sail and tack (zigzag against the wind) if we wanted to continue towards our destination. To my amazement, within a few minutes we were gathering speed again and heading to our destination.

It was at this moment that I realized that many people, who lack a sense of purpose or reason for living, tend to live their lives in a haphazard manner. Whatever way the wind is blowing is where they go. But those that have a sense of purpose for their lives are able to remain on course regardless of the direction of the wind. We need to find a sense of purpose if we are to avoid being distracted by the "winds" of temptation that cry out for our attention. We need a sense of purpose to be able to adjust our course when the wind of change comes across our path. We need a sense of purpose to invigorate us with a sense of excitement, with the anticipation of achieving or goals.

PART II

COGNITIVE CHAIN
OF COMMAND

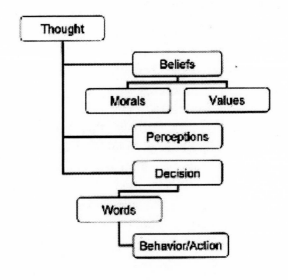

If you are to truly benefit from this book, it is imperative that you understand the cognitive or thought process. With this basic understanding, you will be able to use the R.A.P. principles in your life. The main focus of this chapter will be on recognizing how thoughts influence our decision-making.

As previously stated, mature human beings are responsible for their actions. This means we are also responsible for the processes that lead up to an action. In the chapter on responsibility it was stated that each mature individual is responsible for their thoughts, decisions, words, and actions. If this is true, then it would behoove you to understand the cognitive process. This process is common to us all. I have attempted to simplify the process and make it understandable so you don't have to get your Ph.D to make sense of all this. I have included an illustration entitled "Cognitive Chain of Command" to assist in this endeavor.

The first thing that we need to look at is our thoughts. Thoughts are important because they are responsible for creating mental pictures. They are the catalyst for creating beliefs and perceptions, which will ultimately influence decision-making. With this in mind, you can see the correlation between thoughts and actions. You can make no voluntary action without first thinking, even if it is just for a nanosecond. So, if you can control your thoughts, then you can control your actions. Your thought life is of paramount importance; it is more important than your behavior, due to the fact that it was the thought that created the behavior.

In the Bible Jesus was speaking on the subject of adultery. He made the statement that if a man looked upon a woman with lust in his heart he had already committed adultery with her (Mat. 5:27-28). Jesus knew this principle. He knew that before we commit an act, we first must use our thoughts to create a mental picture. Jesus knew that if we allowed those thoughts to remain in our minds, it would only be a matter of time before we act on those thoughts.

During the course of a day the average person will entertain a myriad of different thoughts. Some of these thoughts are fleeting and unconscious in nature. These types of thoughts we have very little control over. However, some thoughts are self-generated. These thoughts we do have control over. This is important to realize, because it is these thoughts that we will mediate on and eventfully act out.

BELIEFS/PERCEPTIONS

It is from our thoughts that we establish beliefs and perceptions. This is important to understand, for it is your beliefs and perceptions that color your world. For example, if a child is told from an early age that they will never amount to anything by their parents, a belief is established within that child. Most likely, that child will believe that nothing will work out for them. As a result, every opportunity that presents itself will be ignored or avoided due to their perception of themselves. I have encountered individuals that believed that white people were evil and that they could not be trusted. Because of this belief, these individuals look with suspicion every time they interact with a white person.

When I discuss the topic of beliefs and perceptions, I like to use the illustration of a CEO of a corporation. The function of the CEO is to oversee the activities of the corporation. A ranking official within the company may have a great idea, which could be profitable. However, if the CEO is not sold on the idea, it will be left on the boardroom floor. In the same manner, our beliefs and perceptions determine what thoughts we will be receptive to and what thoughts we will reject.

In the illustration provided in this chapter, I placed beliefs higher than perceptions. Both are closely related; however, it is my contention that our beliefs influence our perceptions. If this is true, beliefs would take precedence over perceptions. For example, if you believe that the police are your enemy, then that belief will influence your perception of the police. If a person believes that the police are out to get them, then they will react with a certain sense of apprehension every time they interact with a police officer. Furthermore, their reaction to the police may lead to an unfavorable encounter, which will reinforce that belief. So, in essence, this person has created a self-fulfilling prophecy.

There have been psychological studies done on people who suffer from chronic depression. One of the things that was found with most of these individuals is their ability to pick up negative cues from their environment. In other words, because their beliefs about the world are generally negative, their perception of the world is focused on the negative aspects on life. These are the type of people that will point out all the negatives in a situation without recognizing the positives. This is also true for those who suffer from various forms of conduct disorders, such as being physically aggressive towards others. These individuals generally interpret their environment as being hostile. As result, they will react to their environment in a manner they find appropriate. What is interesting is that others exposed to the same environment fail to view the social cues as either hostile or negative. Similar findings were made with those who suffer from anxiety. (Matthys, Cuperus, & Van Engeland, 1999; Waldman, 1996; Webster-Stratton & Lindsay, 1999)

To illustrate this point even further, I am reminded of a biblical story from the Old Testament involving the nation of Israel. Before entering the promise land Moses, the leader of Israel, sent twelve spies to explore the land and give a report of what they saw. In short, the spies came back and reported that the promise land was a land that flowed with milk and honey. However, only two of the spies believed that they could defeat the people that inhabited the land. The biblical account indicated that ten spies said the following, "We went into the land to which you sent us, and it does flow with milk and honey!" They continued, "Here is its fruit. But the people who live there are powerful and the cities are fortified and very large" (Num 13:27-28a NIV).

Was their report accurate? Yes, but we need to look a little further to see the reason why the ten spies thought they could not succeed in taking the land promised to them. What the scriptures reveal is their self-perception that reflected their belief. The Bible stated, they said, "The land we explored devours those living in it. All the people we saw there are of great size… We seemed like grasshoppers in our own eyes, and we looked the same to them." (Num 13:32b-33NIV) Their belief about themselves influenced their perception of the situation and prevented them from receiving the land promised to them. In addition, their perception prevented others from entering the land as well.

Conversely, two of the twelve spies had a different outlook. They were of the belief that they could take the promise land. The Bible records their statement, "Then Caleb silenced the people before Moses and said, 'we should go up and take possession of the land, for we can certainly do it" (Num 13:30 NIV). It was their belief that gave them a different perception about the situation. What influenced their belief? It is my contention that it was through their relationship with Moses; they acquired a stronger faith in God. According to the scriptures, Joshua accompanied Moses on numerous occasions and was his right-hand man. It should also be noted that Caleb and Joshua were close associates. Here is a saying to mediate on, <u>"What you believe you will ultimately perceive."</u>

Perceptions affect our emotions and attitudes. The person with the "good attitude" is a person whose perception about themselves and the world is generally positive. The reason for this stems from their beliefs about themselves. This self-concept is usually developed in childhood, from various influential sources such as parents, caregivers, and teachers.

DECISIONS

Once a thought is conceived in a person's mind, it is filtered through our beliefs and perceptions. If the thought is able to remain during this process, then it is up to the individual to make a decision on whether to act on the thought. This is where our self-concept, moral, and psychosocial development come into play. If the thought fits where we are psychologically, then we make the appropriate decision to proceed to the next process. If it does not fit, then we make the decision not to proceed. In either case, we are forced to make a decision. Even if we decided to defer a decision, we made a decision.

WORDS

Words are important because they contain our thoughts and allow us to communicate them to others. Words are the conduit that transmits our thoughts to others. How can a person know what you are thinking unless you relate your thoughts to them through your words?

Words paint mental pictures of images in our mind. It is through the use of words we can create images that can change our world. To illustrate this point, I want you to read the following words and see what happens in your thought process.

- **Dog**
- **Big Dog**
- **Big Mean Dog**
- **Big Mean Brown Dog**

If you are like most people when you read the word you did not see the word "dog" in your mind, but you saw an image of a "dog". Maybe it was your dog if you owned one. Or maybe you saw the neighbor's dog. In any event, an image of a dog was created in your mind. With each additional word, the image of the dog changed. If the first image of a dog was a poodle, it probably changed when we got to "big mean brown dog," unless you own a big mean brown poodle. I think you get the point, that our words are tools we use to transmit thoughts and create images.

Words are powerful. They are the most powerful assets we have as human beings. The ability to speak words separates us from other animals on this earth. In the book of James, in the New Testament, the writer, who was the half-brother of Jesus, speaks on the power contained in our mouth. He described our tongue as being a rudder on a large ship, able to turn the ship in any direction it chose. He also described the tongue as being a fire able to burn down an entire forest. (James 3:4-6)

Words are the architect of the soul. With words we can construct a successful and prosperous life, or we can destroy life. In the book of Proverbs it states, "The tongue has the power of life and death, and those who love it will eat its fruit" (Prov 18:21 NIV).

Words are used to direct our lives. It is through our use of words that we determine in what direction our lives will go. If we are faced with an adverse situation and we speak positively to ourselves, we will overcome it. Conversely, if we speak negatively, we will be overcome by it. It is the use of the tongue that determines the outcome, not the situation.

We use words to communicate what we plan to do. When God created the heavens and the earth, did He not imagine it and then speak it (Gen 1:1-31)? Before you decided to go on vacation, enroll in school, change jobs, or buy something, didn't you think it and say to yourself or someone what you planned to do? It is a natural process that we all employ on a daily basis. With this in mind, our words can be used for positive and negative purposes. We can use our words to create or to destroy. We can use our words to build ourselves up, or tear ourselves down. We can also use our words to build others up or tear them down. This is particularly true when it comes to children and those that are emotionally immature. That is why it is imperative that you realize the power you possess in your words.

ACTIONS

Finally, actions are the by-product of our thoughts. Actions are the outward manifestation of our thought life. Actions are reflected in the behavior or attitudes that we display. Actions or behavior reflect to the outer world what we believe about ourselves in relation to our environment. People generally judge us by our actions and or behavior. Many in the field of psychology focus their energy in changing just the behavior. This may be a short-term answer, but if you are unable to get to the root cause, the behavior will manifest itself in a different form. It is my contention that unless you address the thought or belief that is the catalyst of the behavior, you have not resolved the issue.

In summation, if a person wants to change a behavior, they must look beyond the behavior and go directly to the source of that behavior, which is in the mental realm. Change must first start from within the person before it can be manifested on the outside. Change begins with the way we perceive ourselves. What we believe is reflected in what we perceive. As Dr. Albert Ellis stated, "Human beings are largely responsible for creating their own emotional disturbances through the beliefs they associate with the events of their lives." (Ellis 1994)

DISTORTED THINKING

From the last chapter, I hope you realize the importance of your thought life and the power of your words. An increased awareness of this will enable you to create the kind of life you were meant to live. It will give you the ability to become a self-motivated and self-directed individual that will overcome the challenges that life produces. In this chapter, I will discuss some of the common thinking errors I have come across. I like to use the term "distorted thinking" in reference to these thinking errors. Most of these errors or distortions are used by us all, at one time or another. However, when we over-use these thinking errors they can cause us problems.

Have you ever met someone who had a personality problem that caused them difficulty; however, they failed to see that they had a problem? These individuals seem to view others with the problem rather than themselves. I remember when I was in elementary school and was experiencing interpersonal problems with a number of different students. As a result of all the problems I was having, I was sent to the principal's office. The principal sat me down in front of his desk and patiently listened to me as I complained about what everyone was doing to me. After I finished, he asked me one question, "What is the one common element in all the stories you told me about all the people you are having problems with?" I sat there dumbfounded, because I did not have an answer. He finally broke the silence by stating, "It is you." That truth was hard for me to accept at the time, but it made me think. It took several years before I was able to grasp the truth of his statement, but I never forgot it.

What the Principal did was shine the light on a dark spot in my thinking, which was causing me problems. He was performing therapy on my behalf. Unfortunately, I was not very receptive and I wound up coming back to his office several more times. You can say that I had some blind spots in my thought processes.

Blind spots are areas of maladaptive thinking that we are not aware of, or to which we are blind. That is why counseling with a qualified therapist can be valuable; a therapist can point out those areas of thinking that cause us to have problems, which we may not be aware of. Blind spots in our thought processes are generally caused as a result of our beliefs and perceptions. They are also the by-products of the defense mechanisms that we use when faced with traumatic events in our life. According to Sigmund Freud, the father of Psychoanalytic Therapy, ego-defense mechanisms protect an individual from threatening thoughts and feelings. They enable us to soften the blows of emotional wounds and provide a way to maintain an adequate sense of self.

Although defense mechanisms do involve self-deception and distortion of reality, they are not considered essentially pathological or problematic. It is only to the degree in which the individual employs them that they can become a problem. Some of the most recognized forms of defense mechanisms are:

- **Repression is not consciously remembering a threatening or painful thought or desire. By pushing the distressing thought or feeling into their unconscious, the individual is able to manage the anxiety that comes from situations involving guilt or conflict. For example, some adults that were physically or emotionally abused as children will have no recollection of the event that occurred in their childhood.**

- **Denial is similar to repression, but it operates at the conscious level. Like repression,** its function is to suppress unpleasant realities from conscious thought. It attempts to cope with reality by not recognizing the existing anxiety-producing reality. The individual refuses to recognize or accept the reality of the situation they are facing. For example, a person suffers from a substance abuse problem. As a result of their substance abuse issues, they have lost their job and family, however, they refuse to accept that they have a substance abuse problem.

- **Regression** is the returning to a less mature development level. In the face of severe stress an individual will revert to an old behavioral pattern that worked when they were younger. For example, a man begins to act childlike when he is informed that he is being terminated from his job after twenty years of employment.

- **Projection** occurs when a person will attribute their own unacceptable thoughts, feelings, behaviors, and motives to others. They will attribute to others certain feelings and motives that would lead them to feel guilty or uncomfortable if they were to acknowledge that those feeling or motives were their own. An example of this would be the spouse that is involved in an extramarital affair. Quite often they will accuse their spouse of being unfaithful in an attempt to relieve themselves from the guilt of the affair.

- **Displacement** occurs when an emotion is re-directed from the real source to a substitute person or thing. It is usually directed to a person or object that is not threatening. In other words, this is something or someone the person feels is a safe target. A good example of this would be a woman who has experienced a frustrating day at work with her supervisor or fellow employees, and comes home and releases her frustration on her family.

- **Reaction formation** occurs when a person will behave in a manner that is opposite to the way they actually feel. This behavior serves as a defense against the anxiety they would experience if they acknowledged or took ownership of the emotion they actually felt. An example of this would be the person that harbors hostile feelings towards another person; however, they compensate for that feeling by being overtly nice to that person. This behavior attempts to resolve the internal conflict this person is experiencing. This type of behavior is most commonly found in family relationships or interpersonal relationships.

- **Rationalization** is used by a person when they want to justify their actions by imputing some logic or admirable motive to it. From my experience this is the most commonly used defense mechanism. People are good at manufacturing a good reason for their in-

volvement in questionable behavior. There seems to be a propensity towards minimizing the severity of our actions by creating some self-serving logic that makes our action legitimate.

These are just a few of the most commonly used defense mechanisms I have encountered with some of the people I have counseled. As previously stated defense mechanism do have some adaptive qualities to them; however, the misuse and overuse of these mechanisms can become problematic for the user. It is true that defense mechanisms can soften the harshness of reality. However, it only distorts reality rather than changes it. In the long run, the use of defense mechanisms will produce more harm than good. So, accept the responsibility that you possess in dealing with the reality that faces you. Also, remember a problem can only be corrected when it is recognized.

In the next chapter of this book we will discuss how distorted thought patterns can prevent us from achieving what we desire to be or experience. Up to this point I have not given you any homework. Once again, I wanted to lay the foundation of "R.A.P." before we get into any type of exercises to ensure we are all on the same page. However, in this next section you will be required to do some homework if you are to benefit from this chapter. For those of you who like techniques and doing things, you will be happy.

WHAT IS YOUR SCRIPT?

In the last chapter we looked at defense mechanisms commonly used by us all. We also discussed the purpose of defense mechanisms and how misuse of them can hinder our personal growth. In this chapter we will see how negative thought processes are used to sabotage our success.

One of the main reasons that a person fails to live up to their true potential is due to their thought processes. Many people are held hostage by their own dysfunctional thought life. How many times have you witnessed someone that sabotaged his or her own success? I have seen sport teams that appeared to have the game won manage to give the game away. It was as if they had learned how to lose. Week after week this

R.A.P. Therapy For Your Prosperity

team would get a lead, appear to have the won; then all of a sudden, they give the ball away and make one mistake after the other. It was as if they felt they did not deserve to win.

In the same manner some people live their life in the same way. They get a good job and manage to lose it, overcome their substance abuse dependence and fall back into addiction, get out of jail and get off of probation or parole, only to return to jail on a new charge. It becomes a pattern for them.

In most cases these individuals have demonstrated that they possess the skills necessary to maintain a productive lifestyle; however, they fail to overcome the internal demons that keep them from reaching their true potential.

It is our thoughts that ultimately control our emotions and behaviors. If we are to make permanent change, it must start in the mental realm first. Like a computer, we must ensure that we are programming our minds with the right information. As stated in the Bible, "For as a man thinks in his heart, so is he..." (Prov 23:7 NIV). If we spend our days feeding ourselves negative information, how can we expect to produce positive results? So, if your desire is to change what you are experiencing at this present moment, it's time you look at what you are telling yourself on a daily basis.

WHAT IS A SCHEMA?

You might be asking yourself what is a schema? A schema is a psychological term used to describe a particular pattern of thoughts about a certain subject. They are mental templates or frames that represent a person's knowledge about objects, situations, or people. Schemas are useful in simplifying reality or setting up expectations about the probable outcome of a social situation. We use schemas to organize our knowledge, to guide our behavior, to predict likely happenings, and to help us to make sense of our current experiences (Chandler 1997).

I like to think of schemas as a script. When an actor plays a part in a movie he/she are playing a part according to a script, written by a playwright. They study the script and become the individual that the director scripted them to be. In the same manner we live our life according to a script that we or someone else wrote for us.

As mature adults we possess the ability of writing our scripts if we chose, or of accepting the script someone else has written for us. However, children are dependent on their caregivers to provide them with this. That is why it is important that we monitor what we tell our children, especially in the first seven years of their lives because these are the years that they are the most impressionable.

That is why verbal abuse can be so damaging to an individual. As we previously discussed, our words are powerful and can be used to create and destroy. Through our words we can distort a person view of themselves and cause them to feel worthless and helpless. This goes on quite often in domestic violence cases. That is one of the reasons why the victim continues to remain in the abusive relationship, because they believe that no one else wants them and they deserve the abuse. This belief usually comes from either modeling from prior experience or the acceptance of the verbal abuse from the perpetrator.

Why is it that some people always seem to have their act together? They can experience adversity, but somehow they come out of it. It is because they have a schema or script that will not accept anything less. Conversely, there are people that never seem to be able to "pull it together." It does not matter how much help they get, because it's never enough. They will find a way to keep themselves in a rut. Could this be the result of the script that they have accepted for themselves?

At this point I would like you to take some time to see if there are any noticeable patterns in which you find yourself. Do you find yourself always being involved in abusive relationships? How about never being able to "make it over the hump" or getting the break through you have been wanting? Do you always seem to struggle with your finances and never quite have enough to make ends meet? Could it be that you are not allowing yourself to succeed because of your belief about yourself? Only you can answer that question. What script have you written for yourself?

HOW DO YOU WRITE A SCHEMA?

Schemas are developed through our interaction with our environment, or prior experiences.   Dr. Erik Erickson, who has been credited with developing the theory of psychosocial development, was a student in Vienna's Psychoanalytic Institute in the 1920's. He later immigrated to the United States and taught at Yale and Harvard Universities.   It was at this point in his life he became interested in the influence society and culture had on the development of children. In the 1950's he published his first book titled <u>Childhood and Society</u> (Erickson, E.H. 1975).   From his work with children he developed the eight stages of psychosocial development. They are:

- **Trust vs. Mistrust (birth-18 months)**

  The infant must learn to form a first loving and trusting relationship with the caregiver, or develop a sense of mistrust.

- **Autonomy vs. Shame/Doubt   (18 months-3 years)**

  The child's energies are directed towards the development of physical skills, such as walking, grasping, and rectal sphincter control. The child learns control in these areas,

or they are at risk of developing shame and doubt.

• **Initiative vs. Guilt** **(3-6 years)**

The child continues to become more assertive and to take more initiative, but may be too forceful, leading to guilt feelings.

• **Industry vs. Inferiority** **(6-12 years)**

The child must now deal with the demands to learn new skills or risk a sense of inferiority, failure and incompetence.

• **Identity vs. Role Confusion** **(12-18 years)**

The teenager must achieve a sense of identity in occupation, sex roles, politics, and religion. Failure to do this will result in role confusion.

• **Intimacy vs. Isolation** **(19-40 years)**

The young adult must develop intimate relationships or suffer feelings of isolation.

• **Generativity vs. Stagnation** **(40-65 years)**

Each adult must find some way to satisfy and support the next generation.

Erickson summarized that in order for healthy psychosocial development to occur an individual needed to successfully complete each stage of development. If an individual failed to complete a particular stage of development, they would be unable to progress to the next stage of psychosocial development. Erickson's theory of psychosocial development is useful in understanding some of the problems experienced by some in the context of social adjustment. For example, if a person has failed to successfully graduate from the first stage of development, which is trust vs. mistrust, they will have issues with viewing others and their environment in a trusting manner. These individual, generally have problems developing genuine relationships with others because they have learned they cannot trust their environment. Many in the field of psychology are of the opinion that lack of development in this area is the etiology of anti-social behavior.

It is important to understand that there are stages of growth that occur in becoming a mature well-adjusted individual. It just does not happen. That is why being a parent should not be taken for granted. The job of a parent or caregiver is one of the most important responsibilities we have. Furthermore, we will have to give account for what we did or neglected to do in relation to our children. From my experience in the judicial system, I have seen the by-products of improper parenting.

If a child is raised in a nurturing environment and told from birth that they can do anything they put their minds to, and that they will accomplish great things in their life, the probability of that occurring is greatly enhanced. Why? Because the child will develop a cognitive framework that will allow them to progress through all the stages of psychosocial development, which is necessary to be successful in our society. In addition, the ideation of being prosperous will be so inculcated into their thought processes that they will refuse to accept any other ideation which is contradictory. It all goes back to our personal belief system.

Another example of this would be the person that comes from a wealthy family background. Because of their prior life experiences, they have established perception of themselves and the world. As a result, they have certain expectations which shape their reality. They cannot see themselves living in poverty that is not part of their reality. There have been many wealthy people that lost everything they had, but they refused to allow themselves to remain in that condition. These individuals found a way to get back to the status to which they were accustomed. Why? Because their schema would not allow them to accept anything less. There is a big difference in being broke and being poor. Being broke is a temporary state, while being poor is a more permanent state.

The opposite is also true. If a person's schema is that of always being a "loser," they will avoid being successful, and self-sabotage every attempt made toward success. Why? Because their self perception, which is dictated by their schema, will not allow it. That is why it is of paramount importance that you pay close attention to what you say about yourself. Because the words that you speak are writing the script you will ultimately act out in life.

A-B-C THEORY

Now that we have established the importance of having a positive belief system and the nuances between that belief system and the words we speak, we are going to take this one step further. We are going to look at how our beliefs and perceptions can affect our reactions to various situations we encounter in life.

I am going to use the A-B-C Theory established by Albert Ellis, one of the pioneers of Rational Emotive Behavioral Therapy (REBT). Dr. Ellis contends that human beings are largely responsible for creating their own emotional disturbances through beliefs they associate with the events of their lives.

The A-B-C theory of personality and emotional disturbance is the foundation of REBT theory and practice. The theory maintains that it is not the events that have the most impact on the person, but rather the belief about the event, that has the greatest impact on a person. Ellis' contention is that when (A) an activating event occurs, it is not the event which causes (C) the emotional consequence, although it may contribute to it. It is the belief system (B), the belief that a person has about the event that mainly causes (C). Sounds kind of confusing? Let me give you an example. Let's say that a person is passed over for a promotion. This would be (A) the activating event. They become upset. This would be the emotional consequence (C). The reason for their being upset could be the belief that they were overlooked and their efforts were not appreciated by the upper management (B). By believing that they did not receive the promotion because they are unappreciated, this person constructs the emotional consequence (C) of feeling rejected and hurt. (Ellis 1994, 1996)

It was not the failure of obtaining the promotion that triggered the emotional response, but rather the belief about why they did not receive the promotion that caused the person to get upset. Why is it that two people can experience the same event and they respond differently? Could their beliefs and perceptions concerning the event dictate how they will respond?

The great philosopher, Epictetus stated, "Men feel disturbed not by things, but by the views they take of them." This concept was first introduced approximately two thousand years ago. William Shakespeare many centuries later would write, "There is nothing either good or bad, but thinking makes it so."

IRRATIONAL THOUGHTS

From the A-B-C Theory, we can see how our beliefs and perceptions will dictate how we respond to events and situations we encounter. It is not necessarily the event that has the most impact but the thoughts we attach to that event. That is why two people can experience the same event, and one will grow from it, while the other falls apart. With this in mind, it would be beneficial to look at some of the irrational thoughts that we might entertain on a daily basis.

Irrational thoughts are the ones that drive us "crazy". They cause us to avoid taking responsibility for our actions and play the victim role. They can keep us in a state of depression, and make us feel helpless.

Irrational thoughts can cause us to misinterpret the actions of others and cause unnecessary conflicts. If we can identify some of these irrational thoughts that might cause us problems, and arrest them, we will greatly benefit from this. Here are some of the most common irrational thought errors:

- **<u>Over generalized thinking.</u> Over generalized statements is the catalyst for many arguments. By using over generalized statements we put people on the defensive, and more importantly, these statements are usually untrue. An example of an over generalized statement would be, "You never listen to me. You always interrupt me. I do all the work. Everybody picks on me." All these statements are over generalizations that can set us up to become anxious and develop conflicts with others. Watch for words such as "never, always, should, everybody, I can't take it anymore, and I can't stand it." All the aforementioned phrases can trigger an adverse emotional response.**

- **<u>Fortune Telling.</u> Fortune Telling is projecting your assumption on a future event. In most cases, we base this assumption on a past event. By doing this we unconsciously create a situation where we allow past events to dictate future ones. In essence, we create a self-fulfilling prophecy. An example of** this would be the person who says, "Things never work out for me. I tried that before and it didn't work."

- **Kitchen Sinking.** This is bringing up old issues from the past. The motivation behind this is to divert attention from the current issue, and regress to past unresolved hurts and pains. This accomplishes nothing. An example of this would be when a person says, "What about that time when you... You did this to me last year." By doing this on a continuous basis, the individual unknowingly builds up unresolved issues, which will lead to further emotional separation.

- **Focusing on a person's past behavior.** Some people live so much in the unresolved issues of the past that they have difficulty living in the present. These individuals fail to acknowledge the positive changes by a person that once offended them. They fail to rid themselves of the old vision of that person and are held captive by their past perceptions of that individual.

- **Closed minded thinking.** People who are closed minded are unwilling to entertain new thoughts about a particular subject or event. They will usually say something like, "Don't tell me anything. I already know about all that. I don't want to hear anymore." Being so stubborn and insistent on one's own opinion can lead to unnecessary conflicts with others. It will also restrict your options and impair personal growth.

- **Preoccupation with perceived injustices.** Blaming others is a way of life for some people. Also, keeping score of slights from others and dwelling on them creates only feelings of hurt and suspicion. Focusing on unfairness is a major contributing factor for anger, resentment, and holding grudges. Who says life is fair anyway? Things happen; get over it! If you hear yourself saying repeatedly, "It's just not fair. They don't like me because I'm _____;" then, you need to shift your focus and concentrate on finding the solution rather than focusing on the problem.

- **Catastrophic thinking.** This occurs when a person takes a problem or issue and makes it into the worst case scenario possible. Then, they will spend the rest of the day trying to resolve a situation that does not exist. This type of thought process will not only cause unnecessary anxiety, but it will cause others to feel apprehensive as well. Remember, approximately 90% of the things we worry about will never happen. What a waste of time and energy.

- **Egocentric thinking.** This is the type of thought process that causes an individual to take everything said to them as a personal attack. Everything seems to be about them. People that are egocentric thinkers unknowingly set themselves up for constant hurt and frustration. They will complain about how someone hurt their feelings by something which they perceived that the other person said. These individual, are also usually closed minded too. As a result, they are unwillingly to listen to or accept clarification on what they perceived as a personal attack against them. This will cause others to alienate themselves from this individual, as a way to avoid unwanted conflict.

- **Entitlement thinking.** This occurs when someone views their way as the right way and the only way. If someone disagrees with them, they usually get upset. The main reason why they tend to get upset is their belief that they are right, and how dare this person question or challenge them. Furthermore, these individuals feel compelled to get you to see things their way. This type of thinking is also based on closed mindedness.

- **Minimizing.** Is the practice of lessening involvement in an offense or situation? This allows an individual to avoid taking responsibility for their actions. This type of individual will have an excuse ready for why they behaved in a certain manner. Usually someone else will be blamed for his or her behavior or actions. This will ultimately keep an individual in a victim type mental-

ity and hamper their personal growth.

Many individuals that I have encountered in the penal system employ this technique to their own detriment.

These are only some of the most commonly used irrational thoughts that we employ. By becoming aware of these thought patterns, we can begin to recognize when we start traveling down the path of negative thoughts and cut them off before they take root. With this understanding, we can begin to develop strategies to combat these negative thought processes and facilitate positive change in our lives. Remember, you are responsible for your thought life, and your thoughts dictate your behavior.

IRRATIONAL BELIEF EXERCISE

Irrational thoughts can create havoc for us emotionally and keep us enslaved to perceived limitations, which only exist in our minds. Read the following statements and write down some the probable behaviors or actions that the individual might make. Then take it one step further and imagine what the person would experience on a daily basis. For example, how would they feel about themselves? How would they get along with others? What kind of mood would they be in most of the time? How much personal fulfillment would they experience?

- If I didn't have such a bad childhood, I wouldn't be in the mess I am in.

- If I don't do what is expected of me, people won't like me. If I refuse, they will be angry with me. So, I owe it to them to do what they expect me to do.

- My mother always told me that I would wind up like my dad. He didn't amount to nothing.

- I can't stop from worrying so much. I guess that I am just an anxious person; it must be in my genes.

- They just don't want me to get ahead because I'm_____. So why even try.

- It is important to me that everyone likes me. Everyone needs to love me and approve of me all the time.

- I guess that I was born with two left feet. I'll never be able to do that.

- I always get sick this time of year.

- If I didn't have bad luck, I wouldn't have any luck at all.

- Nothing ever seems to go my way; so why even try?

If you have taken the time to do this exercise, you should be able to see the correlations and nuances between thoughts, beliefs, and actions. The results of those beliefs produce the outcomes or experiences. Therefore, if you do not like the outcome of your life then, you need to address the thoughts and beliefs, which dictate that particular outcome or experience.

CHANGING DESTRUCTIVE THOUGHT PATTERNS

Hopefully, you are asking yourself the question, "Can I change some of these negative thought patterns?" You must understand that change is a process; it does not happen overnight. But if you are willing to make a commitment to change and are diligent in making corrections, it will happen for you.

The first obstacle to overcome in changing anything is recognizing the need to change. Many people refuse to recognize their shortcomings and are quick to blame others for their problems. This type of self-deception may provide comfort to the person, but it is a false sense of comfort that will ultimately rob them of genuine personal growth and satisfaction.

Since we have established that everything begins in the mental realm, we must be aware of the thoughts we entertain on a daily basis. You must spend time "watching your thoughts". It is a technique used in mediation; only you do not have get into some yoga position to do it. All you have to do is quiet your mind and just allow yourself to look at what you think. It is like watching an event on television. Most people are so busy going here and there, doing this and that that they do not have the time just to relax and catch up on themselves. Eventually, they become robots, programmed to do what others want them to do. The television, radio, and other forms of media dictate how they should spend their money, where they should go, and what they should do. They never stop to question whether what they are being fed makes any sense. Then they wonder why they are so unhappy and stressed out.

A co-worker of mine gave me some advice that I never forgot. He told me to spend at least fifteen minutes a day by myself and just think. That piece of advice has been invaluable to me throughout the years. So I am passing that advice on to you. Find a time and a place where you are alone. Turn the cell-phone off; turn the television off; close your eyes, and allow your mind to wander. You will be surprised what you will discover.

When we find thoughts that are self-defeating, we must challenge them and then dispose of them. Remember you were created as a free moral agent that is self-determining. This means that you have the power to make choices. You might have to use self-talk, which we will cover later to get rid of any unwanted thoughts.

Once you have uncovered a self-defeating or negative thought, you need to replace it with something positive and uplifting. It is not enough to remove the negative thought; all you do is leave a void. It must be replaced with something positive. That is why it is important that you expose yourself to positive reading material that is uplifting. Personally, I find reading the Scriptures is a great source of inspiration. It has stories from which I can learn. It also provides instruction and guidelines for living a prosperous life.

Make it a daily practice of exposing yourself to some sort of positive spiritual readings or material. It could be something as little as a flash card or a calendar with some positive quotations on it. Over a period of time you will notice that your outlook on things will begin to change. By constant exposure you will begin to change your beliefs and perceptions.

Secondly, you must develop a network of resources that will reinforce your efforts for positive change. This means getting together with others that are in the process of making changes in their life. Whatever the issue that you are facing there are groups out there in which you can become involved. If there is not one, then start your own. If you have issues with alcohol, then you need to attend Alcoholic Anonymous meetings, and find a sponsor. If you have recently been separated from an abusive spouse and were a victim of domestic violence, then you need to find groups that deal with the issues of co-dependency. By becoming involved in these groups, you will realize that you are not alone in your struggle. You will also be exposed to individuals that are addressing their issues in a positive manner. This can be a source of inspiration to you. Most importantly, it will hold you accountable. It is the sense of accountability that can assist you when tempted by your personal demons.

I previously mentioned the use of self-talk in relation to monitoring your thoughts. Self-talk is the revealer of what we really think about ourselves. It also plays a major role in the circumstances in which we find ourselves. If you really want to know why you are in the situation you are in, spend some time monitoring the things you say to yourself. I suggest that you take a pencil and a note pad and jot down some of the things you tell yourself. You will be surprised with what you come up with.

SELF TALK

During a group counseling session one of the inmates I was working with made a statement concerning his substance abuse issues. The inmate stated, "I couldn't stop. I knew that I should quit but I couldn't." After a little inquiry I found out that this was his daily mantra, "I am an addict and I can't quit." What this individual was doing, with his negative self-talk, was robbing himself of the power to overcome his addiction. As a result, he continued this destructive behavior pattern even though he wanted to stop. This inmate later admitted that one of the benefits of being incarcerated was that it allowed him to stay clean of drugs. Unfortunately, this person is now in state prison. What a price to pay to stay clean.

This is a classic example of how self talk works. If this person had changed his self-talk, it would have caused a change in his belief system and eventually would have changed his self-perception. The change in perception would have activated some behavioral changes that would have changed the outcome. Instead of spending two more years in prison, this individual would be free in the community, working, involved in some type of treatment for his substance abuse issues, going to school, attending narcotic anonymous meetings, and being a productive member of society.

As I previously discussed, self-talk has a tremendous impact on how we view ourselves. Most people are unaware of the negative comments that they make about themselves. These statements ultimately keep them living a life below what they envision and desire.

According to Dr. Arnold A. Lazarus, one of the pioneers in the field of cognitive behavioral therapy, negative self-talk could lead to negative self-esteem, anxiety, and depression. Dr. Lazarus is of the opinion that our thoughts and perceptions can dramatically influence our mood, attitude, and emotions (Lazarus 1997).

We talk to ourselves continuously in the privacy of our minds. These statements that we make to ourselves can have a dramatic impact on what we experience in life. As previously stated, self-talk can be either positive or negative. Unfortunately, there are many people who are suffering from the negative consequences of their self-talk. They make statements like, "I'm stupid. I'll never be able to do this. Things never seem to work out the way you want them to." These are just a few of the statements that are made. You can probably come up with some more of your own. But you get the point of what I am saying. These statements that we take for granted can produce negative outcomes in our lives.

This negative self-talk will usually lead to producing negative consequences. Self-fulfilling prophecies are a common occurrence. This is mainly due to the individual's belief in their own propaganda, which creates the situation that they fear. Conversely, the opposite is true. Positive self-talk can produce desirable outcomes. Those who sow the seeds of positive thoughts into their mind will reap positive outcomes. Those who plant negative thought seeds will harvest negative outcomes.

Tell yourself often enough that you are a failure, and eventually you will become one. Tell yourself that you will succeed, and eventually you will. You determine whether you succeed or fail by what you say about yourself. You have the power to change the script if you do not like the role that you are currently playing. Unfortunately, there no set number of times or duration before you change your schema. It something you will have to do until it becomes a natural part of your life. The end result will be well worth the time.

REWRITE THE SCRIPT

This is an encapsulation of what we have already covered in the previous section of the text. Below you will find something to incorporate into your lifestyle. These are things that will eventually become part of your daily routine. It is not something that you do for a period of time then stop when the symptoms go away. These are things that have to become part of your daily lifestyle.

- **Read positive spiritual material on a daily basis. Set aside some time to meditate on what you have read, even if it is as little as five minutes. Some time is better than no time.**

- **Begin to speak positive affirmations about yourself. There are many quotations that successful people have written which you can use. The Bible is a great source in this area. You make the choice on what you will use, as long as it is positive and uplifting.**

- **Begin to monitor your self-talk, and arrest and correct any negative comments. Replace those comments with one that is positive.**

- **Rehearse the times in your life when you experienced success and when you felt encouraged.**

- **Look at your failures as set backs and learning experiences. Thomas Edison, who was credited with inventing the light bulb, stated that it took thousands of experiments before he was successful. What would of happen if he quit? Someone else would have come up with the idea.**

- **Be persistent, do not allow the thought of quitting enter your mind. Quitting is not an option for you.**

PART III

ROAD BLOCKS TO THE PROMISE-LAND

We have discussed the basic philosophical foundations of the R.A.P. therapeutic approach. For the remainder of this book we will cover other areas that can hinder a person from achieving all that they have been called to be. I found that there is a big difference between mentally assenting to something versus believing something. When a person mentally assents to something they are merely agreeing. There is no guarantee that they will act on the subject they agree with. On the other hand, the person who believes will act on their belief. In order for any therapeutic process to work, you must be committed to it totally. You cannot say, "Well I'll give it a try." If you go into anything with that type of attitude you will ultimately fail.

Another reason why this therapeutic approach would not work for you is if you continue to:

- **Fail to monitor your thought life**
- **Fail monitor your speech**
- **Be afraid of failure**
- **Have an unforgiving heart**

So, whenever I counsel with anyone, I will always cover these areas to ensure that the abovementioned are properly addressed and modified if necessary. For the remainder of this book I will discuss each one of the stumbling blocks that would prevent you from entering your promise-land.

Since we are responsible for our thoughts, words, decision, and actions, I will begin with briefly discussing the cognitive thought process. I have developed a chart to assist in this area for those of you that like visuals. Then we will move onto self-image and how to change it through self-talk. From there we will look at how the fear of failure can hinder you from moving forward. Then we will finish with looking at how damaging unforgiveness can be to an individual.

WHAT IS STOPPING YOU?

There are many people who have good intentions when it comes to making positive changes in their lives, unfortunately, few of those people achieve their desired goal. They come into counseling sessions saying all the right things, but they fail to follow through on their commitments. Why does this happen? There are numerous reasons for this. It would take volumes of text to cover this one topic; so I decided to pick two of the most common reasons. They are inertia and entropy. Both of these words are commonly used in physics, particularly in the field of thermodynamics. However, I like to use these terms in psychology because they accurately describe what we sometimes do, when it comes to making changes in our lives.

The word inertia originated with Newton's Law of Motion. Inertia is a property of matter whereby it remains at rest or continues in uniform motion unless acted upon by some outside force. Using this term in the context of this book, inertia refers to someone that knows what they should do but fails to act.

Closely related to inertia is entropy. Entropy is the second law of thermodynamics. Simply put entropy is the degree of disorder in a system. If a system operates in an orderly manner it is in a state of (low entropy). Conversely, the more disorder found in a system the higher the degree of entropy. Using this term in the context of this book, entropy refers to someone who starts off in total complinance to their treatment/ rehabilitation program but slowly deviates from the program and eventually reverts to their old behavior pattern. There are a myriad of reasons why a person would experience either of one of these states. However, the common denominator is failure to maintain their vision and motivation.

If you are caught in either of these two categories, you first need to admit it to yourself. Then you need to ask yourself some questions. If you have a plan of action but have yet to act on it, you need to ask yourself why. Review the reasons listed, and find the one that fits your situation. If you have started on a plan of change but have quit, you need to re-kindle the flames of motivation that got you started. You need to remember the reason why you wanted to change, and recreate the vision you once had. Making changes is not easy. If it were, everyone would do it.

Here are some other reasons I have found most common in people who fail to follow through on their commitment for positive change:

- **Laziness. Some people just are not willing to put forth the effort necessary to make and sustain positive change. Most difficulties that we have did not occur overnight; they took time and effort. Unfortunately, it will take just as much or more effort and time to rectify the situation. Most people are looking for the quick fix.**

- **Lack of motivation. Some people find it difficult to get motivated long enough to make and sustain change. They lack the ability to be self-motivated. These individuals are looking for someone to motivate them. If that person is not there they will quickly regress to their previous state.**

- **Fear. Some people have become comfortable with their circumstances, even though they dislike where they are. They become fearful of the thought of changing their situation. They are enslaved by their fear of the unknown.**

- **Learned helplessness. Some people have learned to be dependant on others, and** would rather remain in that situation, than become independent. These individuals lack the confidence to be on their own and self reliant.

- Lack of faith. Some people question whether they are capable of making positive changes in their life, and are lacking in the spiritual aspects of life.

- Procrastination. This occurs when a person deliberately postpones action to a plan they may have developed or which someone else had developed for them. The reasons for this procrastination could be: a lack of faith in their ability, fear of change, lack of motivation, or learned helplessness.

- Complacency. Some people may have the ability to change but lack the commitment to put forth the effort necessary for change. As a result, they fall into a state of complacency. "I will do it tomorrow."

- Conflicted agenda. This occurs when a person may want to change; but if the change occurs, it would cause some type of internal conflict. These individuals will start the process of change, and then suddenly regress to a previous behavior for no apparent reason. An example of this would a person who was raised to believe having an abundance of money was evil. This person may not like their current financial status, and may even make attempts to elevate him or herself;

however, unless they deal with the belief that money is evil, they will experience internal conflict every time they achieve a measure of success in this area.

IF WISHES WERE HORSES, BEGGARS WOULD RIDE.

The key ingredient for change is having a strong belief system. Because change is difficult, many people do not possess the strength of character to see the entire process through. It takes a strong belief and vision to see your dreams become reality. There will be plenty of opportunities for you to give up along the way, and many do. With this in mind I want to look at another aspect necessary to completing your goal, and that is being able to distinguish the difference between wishing, wanting, and believing.

I have found that merely having a desire to accomplish something is only the beginning of the process. It takes more than just desire to achieve a goal. Many people do not take the time to allow their desire to grow within them, to the point it becomes strong enough to sustain them throughout the entire process. That is where having a purpose or reason for completing the task comes into play.

What I have found is three basic categories of people that desire change. The first group of people is what I call the "wishers". They will say some thing like, "I wish that things would get better," or, "I wish that I could do that." Do these individuals desire to change? Yes. But, they have not established a strong enough belief system to even go beyond expressing a desire to change. Most of the time their efforts stop right after they express their desire. Unfortunately, these individuals will live the rest of their lives in a state of inertia.

The next group of people is what I call the "wanters." The "wanters" unlike the wishers will actually put forth some efforts to accomplish their goals. They will say something like, "I think that I am going to try to do it." or, "I want to lose some weight this year." However, these individuals will usually fall by the wayside at the first sight of adversity. You see the "wanters" at gyms every year. They will make a New Year's resolution to get back into shape. They buy the membership, clothing and get a training routine going. They are going regularly to the gym in the month of January, but when March and April comes around, they begin to come sporadically. By May, they are nowhere to be found. Why does this occur? They did not allow their desire for change become strong enough. They lost their vision and the reason why they started the program. They had no purpose or vision.

The last group of people is what I call the "believers." The "believers" have developed a concrete vision of what they want to accomplish. As a result, they are able to maintain the reason or purpose why they want to accomplish whatever it is they are seeking. They will endure the hardships and disappointments until their desire comes to fruition.

What is important to note is that all three groups had a desire for change, but only one group actually experienced success. The moral of the story is that it takes more than desire to make things happen. You must couple that desire with a strong belief, which will give you the confidence that it will happen. Once this occurs, your belief turns into knowing that it will happen. Once you know something is going to happen, you are able to endure whatever is placed before you because you know that whatever it is you want will ultimately happen.

With belief comes power. Jesus stated to his disciples, "I tell you the truth, if anyone says to this mountain, 'Go throw yourself into the sea', and does not doubt in his heart but believes that what he says will happen, it will be done for him." (Mark 11:22 NIV) Belief causes us to create a knowing within us necessary to achieve our goals.

In order to change your believing into a sense of knowing something is going to happen, you must have a strong belief system. This is where people who have a belief system that includes a Spiritual Source are at an advantage. The reason I say this is because I have found that there are times when I need a source of power outside of myself. As a human being, there are limitations on our ability. However, with God there are no limitations. Being able to call upon that power in times of need is not only comforting, but it gives me a sense of confidence that I would not be able to experience without a belief system that did not include God.

When Bill Wilson and Dr. Bob Smith started Alcoholics Anonymous, it was the result of a spiritual experience Wilson had with God in a hospital room. Wilson was a recovering alcoholic who had relapsed. As result of his relapse he was hospitalized. While in his hospital bed he had a spiritual encounter with God. He ultimately allowed God to become part of his life. He had what some would call a spiritual awakening. Even though he still had cravings to drink, he found the strength to fight those cravings.

It was through this spiritual awakening that the concept for Alcoholic Anonymous was born. Bill contacted his friend Dr. Smith, who also was struggling with his

IF WISHES WERE HORSES BEGGARS WOULD RIDE.

alcohol addiction, and he found that being able to talk to someone about his cravings was not only comforting but it took away the craving. From this experience they agreed to meet regularly to talk openly about their addiction.

From their initial meetings together, Mr. Wilson and Dr. Smith recruited others with alcohol addiction issues. As the group became more successful additional groups were established. Bill Wilson then felt the need to write down some guidelines and instructions on how the meetings should be conducted. From this desire he dictated the first chapters of the Twelve Steps Program. However, he met some resistance when he mentioned God so much in the text. Bill refused to omit God from the twelve steps, but added the phrase, "God as we understand him," as a concession. That is where the term "higher power" originated. What is the concept of the higher power? It is the source of power outside of you. The belief in a power source outside of our limited abilities has been the catalyst for many great human achievements.

To explain this process by using the cognitive chain of command model, let's start with the desire or thought. The thought or desire enters the mind. At that instant we have the ability to dismiss or meditate on the thought or desire. If we chose to meditate on the thought, it is filtered through our cognitive thought process, which includes the belief and perception components.

Once the desire is allowed to continue in our cognitive process, mental pictures and images are created. We then begin to visualize the desire in our conscious and subconscious mind. It is at this point that the desire is conceived in the mental realm and begins to grow. From that moment on it grows until the desire is ready to manifest itself in the physical realm. This process is much like the same process that a woman goes through when giving birth to a child. Think of the desire being the sperm, the imagination as being the fertile egg, and the mind as being the uterus.

I would like to leave you with another example I often use from the Scriptures. It is a story about Abram, who would later be called Abraham. God had promised Abram that he would have a son. This promise was given to him when he was seventy-six years old. On top of that he and his wife Sarai, later known as Sarah, was unable to have children (Gen 12:1-9). Abram later questioned God about the promise He had given him. God again told Abram that he would have a son from his wife, but this time he told him to do something. He told Abram to look at the stars in the sky and count them because that would be the number of his offspring (Gen 15:1-5). In essence, God was teaching Abram how to visualize. Unfortunately, Abram compromised and attempted to help God out, through the encouragement of his wife. But twenty-two years later Sarai did finally give birth to a child. His name was Isaac.

It is important to realize that it takes time to make your dreams become reality. It is imperative that you spend time everyday rehearsing the visions of what you want to accomplish. Visualize what you want to do. Establish within yourself valid reasons for achieving the goal. Also make positive affirmations to yourself in relation to the achievement of that goal. Most importantly, look to a source outside of yourself to empower you. By doing this you will greatly enhance your chances for success.

RESPONSIBILITY FOR YOUR FUTURE

The major obstacle most of my clients had to overcome was realizing that they were responsible for their successes or failures. They could not blame their mother, father, bother, sister, homeboy, dog, or the cat for their predicament. That is why I introduce the principles of R.A.P. in the beginning of every counseling session. It provides the foundation necessary to keep everyone from becoming victims. If you are a victim, then you are not responsible for what has happened to you.

It is my intent to empower the individual to take charge of his/her life. This can only happen if the person understands that they have to assume responsibility for their thoughts, decisions, words, and actions. Having this frame of mind will keep you from the victim mentality and propel you to one of empowerment and self-reliance. In other words, the person is operating from an "internal locus of control".

The term "internal locus of control" refers to a person's ability to assume responsibility for their circumstances. They realize that they have the resources within themselves to make changes when necessary. Though they may seek the assistance of others, they do not rely solely on others to make changes for them. This leads to self-reliance.

Being responsible and taking control of your life allows you to sit in the driver's seat of your destiny rather than being a passenger. Some people find this thought frightening. They have become accustomed to others making those choices for them. That way they can blame them for their circumstances. They can blame them for their unhappiness. They can blame them for their lack of achievement. These types of people simply absolve themselves from taking any responsibility for their situation. This type of individual operates from an "external locus of control".

The term, "external locus of control" refers to a person's unwillingness to assume responsibility for their circumstances. They fail to acknowledge that they have the resources within themselves to make changes when necessary. They rely solely on the assistance of others to make changes for them. This leads to dependency on others.

In order to be successful in this society, one must have a certain degree of independence and self-reliance. This means having the ability to operate within one's own scope of power. Most employers crave employees that have the ability to be self-motivated and are able to take the initiative to solve problems on their own. Our society rewards those who have the courage and vision to come up with new ideas and solutions for existing problems. Major corporations welcome those who use their resources to come up with innovations that can provide service to society and produce income. I challenge you to read the biographies of some of those who are successful. What you will find in most cases are people who were self-motivated and operated from an internal locus of control.

A responsible person understands the power of their decisions. Your decisions of yesterday have placed you in the position you are in today. You must realize that in order to live a fruitful and productive life, you must learn to make the proper decisions at the right time.

LEARN TO GO WITH THE FLOW

You have developed your plan of action. You have spent time visualizing the results, and all of a sudden, unforeseen circumstances arise. The job you thought you would get falls through. The relationship you hoped would be restored does not happen. The money you were promised does not materialize. You think to yourself, "Why is this happening to me? Maybe

God does not want me to succeed. Maybe all this stuff about changing is a bunch of ____. Maybe my friends were right. The system is designed to keep us down. Why try anyway? I was better off the way I was."

Life is not fair! Things happen over which we have no control. Why this happens to some people and not to others is a mystery that we can contemplate on for the rest of our lives. As I previously stated, it is not what happens to us that matters; it is how we react to it. It is the person who is able to adapt to their circumstances that will be the most successful. To adapt means the ability to alter your plans according to the situation that faces you.

In the field of sports, it is the coach who is able to make adjustments during the course of a game and season that will be successful. From my involvement in sports, I observed that it was not the coach who had the best game plan that always won the game. All competitive teams have a game plan. Coaches spend weeks developing a game plan for each opponent they will face in the course of the season. But it is the coach that is able to make adjustments to their opponent's game plan that will win the game. Coaches that are unable to make adjustments will be at a disadvantage and may lose games to teams with lesser talent.

In order to make proper decisions, you have to look at all the options or opportunities you have. Many people do not do this. They limit themselves to just a few options, when in reality they had many more options available to them. They unknowingly put themselves into a "box." What successful people have learned to do is to think outside of the "box." Those in the business field will often have what they call, "brainstorming sessions." During these sessions the participants are encouraged to share their opinions and ideas in solving a particular problem. With each proposed idea other are invited to look at the positives and the negatives of the idea. From this process the group collectively arrives at the best solution or idea for addressing an issue.

It would greatly benefit us to use this method when faced with important decision-making. Take time to sit down and write out all the options you can think of regarding a particular situation that you are facing. From this list of options write out the positives and the negatives of each one you have come up with. Also incorporate the principle of accountability. What is the impact on others if you choose a particular option? Are you willing to live with the consequence of that decision? Remember that we all have to give account to someone for our behavior on this planet. Finally, what is the purpose or reason for choosing that particular option? This is how you can use the principles of R.A.P. in a practical way in making decisions.

COUNTING THE COST

Another common obstacle that keeps a person from making positive change is not realizing the cost of change. Making changes in one's life can be stressful. You are talking about changing old behavior patterns with which you have become somewhat comfortable. It is no wonder why some many people revert back to their old behaviors after feeling the stress of change. That is why it is important to constantly bring to remembrance the motivation for the change. What is the reason or the purpose that motivated you in the beginning? This will recreate the vision you had and give you hope and encouragement.

Always remember that it is normal to feel uncomfortable when you initially start something that is new and unfamiliar. When you switch to a new job, move into a new neighborhood, or start new relationships, it is going to take time before you feel comfortable.

As previously stated, there are a myriad of reasons why people fail to complete the process of change. But the one that is seldom discussed is the effort that is needed for the change. Counselors/Therapist do a great disservice to their clients when they do not inform them of the personal cost change requires. There are many self-help books out there that make it seem easy. Just do this, that, and the other, and you will be fine. I wish it were that easy, but it is not. To make permanent change takes persistence and effort. You must be committed. If you are not committed to making change, it will not happen for you. I do not care how many therapists, psychologists, or psychiatrist you see. If you do not commit yourself to doing what is necessary to change, you are just wasting your time and money. Anyone who tells you anything different is not being honest with you.

How do you become committed? It goes back to establishing a purpose or reason for making change, and then creating a vision in your mind of what you plan to accomplish. If it is getting clean and sober so that you can get on with your life, see yourself clean and sober. Remember times when you were clean and sober and enjoying yourself. If it is re-uniting with your family, see yourself re-united with your family again. Remember the good times you had with your family. If is getting back on your feet financially, see yourself working with money in the bank paying your bills on time. See yourself owning that home you wanted. See yourself making wise investments with your money and watching it grow. These mental images and visions will help you endure the birthing process that change requires.

Finally, it is important to remember that the bigger the goal the longer it will take to manifest itself in the physical realm. Remember the analogy I used for the conception of a dream or vision. The desire is the seed or sperm, the imagination being the fertile egg, and the mind is the uterus. The normal birthing process for the conception and birth of a human is approximately nine months. However, the same process for an elephant is approximately a year and a half. The point that I am trying to make is that there is generally a correlation between the size of our dreams and the time it takes for them to manifest, but there are always exceptions to the rule.

What I have found helpful and recommend to others is setting smaller goals that will ultimately lead to the bigger goal. For example, if you wanted to become a lawyer but never finished high school, there would be some other steps you would need to complete before being eligible to take the state bar exam. You would have to either go back to school to obtain your high-school diploma or equivalent. Then you would need to probably attend a community college to obtain the credits necessary to be eligible to attend a four-year college. You then need to graduate from the college with high enough grades that would make you eligible to attend law school. Once accepted into law-school, you need to graduate. Finally, once you graduate you need to pass the bar exam. This entire process will take anywhere from seven to ten years. That is a long time.

Setting individual goals along the way makes the journey encouraging and fulfilling. Everyday will be a new adventure. With each accomplished goal along the way, your confidence will grow, and you will feel better about yourself. With this confidence you will realize the treasures that life has for those willing to search for them.

As has been my practice, I would like to leave you with a personal story of how I employed these techniques in my life. My wife is an avid runner. She regularly runs and has run several marathons. I too like to run but not that long of a distance. I would regularly run distances between one and half to two miles, maybe once or twice a week. The other days I prefer to do weight training.

After watching her train for a marathon, the thought of running that distance entered my mind. I knew I could do it if I wanted to. But did I want to pay the price it would require? I knew that I would have to put in at least 40-70 miles a week in running. This would mean that I would have to give up some time in the gym. After some thought I decided that running a marathon at this time was not for me, maybe a shorter distance.

I decided that running a 10K (6.2 miles) or half marathon was a more realistic goal for myself. I pondered on the idea for several months until a friend of mine suggested that I run with him in a 10K. It was funny that he invited me to run with him because I had never mentioned my secret desire to him of running a 10K. I took it as a sign from God to run the race.

I asked my friend what I should do to prepare for the upcoming race, and he suggested that I increase the distance I was running to get my body used to running for longer periods of time. Not taking his advice too seriously, I increased my runs from two miles to four miles. I rationalized that if I could run four miles, I should not have any problems running six miles. How wrong this reasoning turned out to be.

On the day of the race I looked in vain for my friend but could not find him. So I had to run alone. I started out the race with a moderate pace. I did not want to start out too fast and burn myself out, and I did not want to run too slowly either. For the first several miles I felt pretty comfortable and was beginning to pass some people. I would estimate I was in the upper half of the five hundred people that were running.

With every stride I was becoming more confident that I would achieve my goal of finishing the race in under an hour. Everything was going fine until I reached mile four. All of a sudden I felt twitches in my thigh muscles. Then I began to feel tightness in my lower back. I tried to ignore the pain, but with every step I took the pain became more intense. I argued with myself mentally. One side of my brain was saying stop before you seriously hurt yourself. The other side was saying you can do it, don't stop. Finally, the side of my mind that said stop won. I said to myself, "I will just walk for a few steps; then, I'll begin to run and finish up strong."

The few steps turned into a mile and a half. I would run a few steps, feel my legs start to cramp, and stop, and walk again. All those people that were behind me started passing me offering encouragement as they continued. Finally, when I could see the finish line, I began to jog slowly and crossed it after one hour and twenty minutes. Needless to say, I was a little discouraged with my time, but I learned from that experience. I knew that if I wanted to achieve my goal, I would have to make some adjustments in my training.

I used that experience as a catalyst for change. It motivated me to increase my knowledge base on distance training. It also provided me with the spark I needed to meet my ultimate goal of running a half marathon. To make a long story short, I found another 10K race. This time I trained with more purpose and dedication. Nine weeks later I ran another 10K; only this time I was ready for the challenge. I not only finished the race without stopping, but I knocked off nearly twenty minuets from my previous time. Later that same year, I ran my first half-marathon.

From this example you can see the principle articulated to you in this chapter. First, there was the idea. Then, was the filtering of the idea by my belief and perceptions. Next, followed by the desire and the conception of that desire. This was followed by the action, the manifestation of the desire, and the realization of the goal. No matter what your goal may be, the process is the same. What you believe, you can achieve.

YOUR PAST AND YOUR FUTURE

Another major hindrance that I have found is the inability of letting go of the past. Some people are not able to move forward because they are held captive to their past. I cannot count the times I have heard someone blame their current situation on some past event that occurred a number of years ago. My question to them is, "What does something that happened to you twelve years ago have to do with right now?" Absolutely nothing! It's like seeing a man wearing a raincoat during the heat of summer with not a cloud in the sky. When you ask him why he is wearing the raincoat, the man precedes to tell about a situation that occurred in March. In March this man was walking to work when all of a sudden it started to rain. Because he did not have his raincoat or umbrella, he got soaking wet. After that experience the man said that would never happen to him again so he has worn his raincoat everyday since. It does not matter what the weather conditions are; he is going to wear his raincoat.

Most people would think that the actions of this man are rather foolish. But there are people who live their lives like this man. They refuse to let go of some painful event of the past. As a result, it interferes with their present and future. Image how uncomfortable you would feel walking around in a bright yellow raincoat in ninety-degree weather. Well, that is the way some people feel everyday for no apparent reason. Everyone else is enjoying the sunshine, making themselves comfortable, and here is this person sweating profusely and complaining about the heat. All they have to do is take off the raincoat and they would feel more comfortable.

One of the main reasons why some people have problems maintaining their effort towards positive change is because they fail to create a new image of themselves. They continue to see themselves the way they were. This ultimately results in them regressing back to their prior state. This is what I referred to as a "conflicted agenda".

If a person has issues in the past with which they have not dealt with, it can prevent them from fully enjoying their present and future. What occurs is that the person creates a conflicted agenda within him/herself. They want to change, but something within them keeps that from happening. For example, a woman looks at herself in the mirror and has noticed she has put on some weight. She looks in her closet at all the clothes she used to wear but cannot wear now because she does not fit into them anymore. She later goes to the shopping mall and sees new outfits that she would like to buy, but they have none of those outfits in her size. Frustrated she makes the decision that she going to lose the weight and get down to the size she was in college.

She starts going to gym and watching her diet. She continues her new weight reduction program for six months and starts seeing positive results. She now begins to fit into some of the clothes she could only dream of wearing a year ago. The woman achieved her goal of wearing a size seven. She also notices that she is getting attention from the opposite sex. Men that used to pass her by are now giving her a second look and asking her out for dates. Though she likes the attention, it makes her uncomfortable.

With the more attention she receives from men, the more uncomfortable the woman becomes. Finally, she stop going to the gym and disregards her diet. Within a matter of several months she not only gained back the weight she lost but put on ten additional pounds. It turned out that ten years ago this woman was raped. At that time she was a size seven and was quite physically attractive.

Because she had never completely recovered from the trauma of the rape, when she returned to the weight and clothing size of that event, she began to feel discomfort. She started re-living the event in her mind. She created visions of the same thing happening again.

To protect herself from the imaged rape, she decides to make herself unattractive to men again. Even though she does not like the way she looks, she lives with it because she feels uncomfortable being physically attractive to men. This is an example of a "conflicted agenda," wanting something but not allowing yourself to obtain it because of an unresolved issue that occurred in the past. Is something in your past robbing you from creating a brighter future?

ARE YOU INSANE?

One of the best definitions that I heard for insanity is, "Doing the same thing over again and expecting to get different results." If it did not work for you the last time, what makes you think that this time will be any different? Unfortunately, I have seen individuals waste the most productive years of their lives with this type of mentality. They say something like, "Well, next time I won't get caught." What they fail to acknowledge is that this is the tenth time they made this statement!

Like the person who has unresolved issues lingering in their past which prevents them from progressing forward, so are those who refuse to let go of unproductive ways of doing things. If it has not worked for you in the past, why do you think it will work now? Some people are so prideful that they would rather suffer hardships than admit that they are wrong.

Some people would rather collect unemployment than find a new line of work because they only see themselves doing one kind of job. Some people, who have the talent and skills to be successful in business, would rather make money by illegitimate means because they view themselves as being a "gangster" or hustler. Being successful sometimes requires us to make changes in the way we see ourselves and do things. Sometimes we have to admit that our old thought patterns and behaviors are not in our best interest. This requires that we humble ourselves and swallow our pride. If we are not willing to do that, we will not be able to progress any further.

I am reminded of the story of the Nation of Israel when Moses led them out of Egypt. For four hundred years, the Egyptians oppressed them; and finally the Hand of God, through Moses, miraculously delivered them. The journey to the "promised land" was to take approximately eleven days. However, because of their unbelief and disobedience, it took forty years! As a result, most of the people that started towards the "promised land" never made it there; they died in the wilderness.

Like the Nation of Israel, many of us have been afforded the opportunity to leave our wilderness experience and venture into the promised land of a brighter future.

But in order for that to happen, we must be willing to let go of the things of the past that hinder us and keep us enslaved. We must exercise faith, look at all of our options, and be willing to change thoughts and behaviors that have proved to be detrimental to us in the past.

God has provided us all with the ability and opportunity to change the path we travel. It is just a matter of choosing to look for it. There are people that believe they cannot change; so they do not. There are some people that believe that they are destined for a certain type of lifestyle, and they do nothing to change their fate. But there are those who realize that change is possible, no matter how "impossible" it may appear. These are the people who reap the benefits of what life has to offer. Which category are you in right now, and are you willing to change to reach your promised land?

ANGER AND HOW TO DEAL WITH IT

Anger is a normal part of life. The Bible records that even Jesus got angry and chased the moneychangers out of the Synagogue (Matt 21:12-13). The Bible also acknowledges that we will experience anger while in this world. From the New Testament book of Ephesians it states, "In your anger do not sin, and do not let the sun go down while you are still angry" (Eph 4:26 NIV). From both of these examples we see that being angry is not the problem is what we do with that anger.

Many people associate anger with being negative, but anger can be used for positive purposes. In the case of Jesus, he used his anger to address the misrepresentation and exploitation, which the religious leaders were perpetuating against the people in the name of God.

It was anger that motivated people to fight against the social injustices in this country during the 1960's. But there is a fine line between the positive and negative aspects of anger. In this chapter we will look at what anger is and how it can be a hindrance to our personal growth.

WHAT IS THE SOURCE OF ANGER?

Anger is actually a secondary emotion. In other words, the emotion of anger is the result of another emotion. There are basically four primary emotions that can cause someone to experience anger. They are fear, frustration, loss, and hurt/disappointment. At the core of anger are unfilled expectations. Someone says something we do not like, does not do something we expected or something happens that we did not expect. These can all cause us to experience anger.

According to Charles Bass, the author of the book entitled, Banishing Fear from Your Life, people often use anger to deal with fear. Bass stated, "The process by which fear provokes anger is relatively simple: we use anger to cope with fear".

UNRESOLVED ANGER & THE CONSEQUENCES

Dr. Howard Markman of Denver University, one of the leading experts in the prevention of divorce, gives strong warning about allowing anger to remain hidden.

He suggests that those unresolved issues accumulate within us and become a combustible combination if left unattended for too long. Some of the consequences of allowing unresolved anger to reside in us are the following:

- **Distance from others. When anger is deep felt and unresolved, the natural response is to distance ourselves from others. There is this natural tendency not to let others get close to us. In essence, it blocks our ability to give and receive love.**

- **Distance from God. This occurs in the form of spiritual blindness. As the Bible clearly states, God is love (1 John 4:8). If we harbor hatred in our hearts towards others, we give no place for God to reside within us. That is why we are instructed in the scriptures to forgive those who trespass against us. (Matt 6:14-15). This prevents unresolved anger to reside within us. By doing this, we allow God the ability to work in our belief and answer our prayers (Mk 11:22-25).**

- **Distance from yourself. Another consequence of unresolved anger is a lower sense of self. Quite often when a person is mistreated, they will initially feel hurt, frustration, and sometimes fear. However, later those emotions evolve into anger. In most cases, this anger is turned inward and manifests itself in a form of anxiety or depres-**

sion.

- **Distance from maturity. Unresolved anger can freeze us at a certain level of emotional maturity. This usually occurs at the level of maturity of the individual at the time of the offense. For example, if a child experiences an emotional painful event at age eleven, and that issue is not addressed properly, that child will be greatly hindered in their emotional development, from that point on. They may be developed in other areas of their life, but their emotional development will be hindered.**

Unresolved anger is like having a tape recording of the unresolved offense running in your mind. This constant rehearsing of the offense not only causes damage to the individual but also to those that are around them. If we do not learn how to let go of unresolved anger, we will open ourselves to being enslaved to it. I will briefly describe some techniques that I have found helpful in releasing unresolved anger. Most of this information I found in a book written by Gary Smalley, which is entitled, <u>Making Love Last Forever</u>. I highly recommend that you get a copy of this book!

1. **Determine what upset you. You need to be able to articulate what happened that caused you to get upset. If possible write the offense down and be as specific as possible.**

2. Give yourself permission to grieve. It is not only natural but also imperative that you allow yourself the opportunity to grieve. This is very therapeutic. By grieving you are accepting the reality of the loss and pain. By not allowing yourself to grieve, you delay the healing process.

3. Try to understand the offender. This is probably the most difficult thing to do. But by doing this it will speed up the healing process and gives us the ability to avoid holding resentment towards that individual. By understanding why the offender acted the way they did, we will be able to empathize with them, and be in a better position to forgive them.

4. Release the offender. We must forgive and let go of the desire to get revenge if we want to free ourselves from the contaminating affects of unresolved anger and find peace. I know that this runs counter to the philosophy of this world. One of the major components of releasing or forgiving someone is giving up the idea that they have seen the errors of their ways.

   This may never occur. If we forgive under the condition that we receive an apology, we are setting ourselves up for another let down.

5. Look for pearls in the situation. We can learn from just about every situation we

come across, if we choose to do so. When we do this, we attach meaning to the experience, and it becomes profitable to us. It also positions us where we can assist others who are going through a similar situation.

6. Put your feelings into writing. One of the best ways I have found to release pent up frustration and anger is to write what I feel on a piece of paper. By expressing your feelings of hurts, frustrations, and fear, you release the anger attached to those emotions. Writing a letter to the offender telling them what you feel is very therapeutic. It does not matter if you send the letter; it is the act of writing out your feelings that is important.

7. Reaching out to the offender. This is by far the most difficult to do. This involves the act of the will and requires a high degree of maturity. When someone has hurt us through an offense, we generally feel betrayed. There are issues of trust that need to be addressed. Sometimes the relationship we had with that person will never be the same. We may never be able to recapture the emotions we once had for that person, but we can treat them the way we would like to be treated. Do not allow your emotions to dictate to you whether you have forgiven someone. Forgiveness is an act of your will; the emotion will follow.

Having unresolved anger within us has many detrimental effects. Refusing to acknowledge that we have unresolved anger causes us to harbor resentment towards those who have offended us. This resentment can have adverse effects on us emotionally as well as rob us of the personal peace and contentment we seek. Some people waste precious time devising ways to seek revenge in an attempt to "get even", thinking that it will give them some sort of happiness. The reality of the situation is that it does not. They also suffer from the inability to live in the present. People with unresolved anger are not able to completely enjoy their current relationships because of their pre-occupation with past events. They suffer from being held captive to the past. They suffer from not being able to find peace within themselves. Forgive and release those who have hurt you, so that you can be released from the prison of unresolved anger.

YOUR SUCCESS DEPENDS ON YOU

I hope that you have found this book helpful in your quest for self-empowerment. Those that are the achievers in life are those that realize they are responsible for their decisions and actions. We have been created to be self-determining, with the power to make choices. If we use this power wisely, it can benefit us; if it is used unwisely, it could ultimately destroy us.

When you realize that you are responsible for your thoughts, decisions, words, and actions, you understand that you are responsible for the situations in which you find yourself. This realization can be empowering. The reason for this is that if you do not like where you are, you have the power to change the situation. From this mindset you are in a position to live your life from an internal locus of control, not allowing outside circumstances to dictate your outcome.

With the understanding of what it means to be responsible, you also want to incorporate the principle of being accountable. Accountability assists us in empathizing with others, which causes us to consider the feelings of others prior to making decisions that would be detrimental to them. It also helps us to regulate our behavior because we realize that our actions <u>do</u> affect others, and we <u>will</u> ultimately be held accountable for what we did or did not do.

Finally, you need to have a sense of purpose for your life. Having a sense of purpose gives us a reason to live. It invigorates us with hope when we get tired. It can inspire us when the external pressures that accompany this life come against us. Purpose can put the pep in your step and the glide in your stride when others around you are stumbling around on the wayside.

With responsibility, accountability, and purpose, you must have the courage to look at yourself and examine your beliefs and thought processes. Are your beliefs keeping you from the happiness and prosperity that you seek? Is there unresolved anger and resentment that is short-circuiting and undermining your efforts to progress? If so, then you must be willing to address those issues and make the proper adjustments. If you find areas of conflict that stand in the way of your success, they need to be removed. If you find yourself involved in negative self-talk, you need to address and change that talk with positive self-talk. Remember change is a process that requires effort! You must be willing to put forth the effort necessary to complete the process.

Change requires us to make a commitment. You must be willing to commit yourself to your plan to succeed. If you are willing to do what is necessary to make changes in your life, it will happen for you. It might take some time; old habits and thought patterns are hard to overcome, but with faith and persistence anything is possible. Just make up your mind that you are going to play the game until you win.

To assist you in the area of commitment I have included a copy of the contract I use with my clients. This contract is to be signed and reviewed on a daily basis. Look at it first thing in morning and before you go to bed at night. Read it to yourself to remind yourself to renew your commitment to positive change.

A CONTRACT WITH MYSELF

As part of my commitment to happiness and prosperity I agree and endorse the following:

- **I proclaim to live life to my fullest potential.**

    _____ (initial)

- **I will daily monitor my self-talk and make positive statements concerning the obtainment of the goals that I have set for myself, until they come to fruition.**

    _____ (initial)

- **I realize that there exists a tendency within me to become discouraged and depressed, but I will not be controlled by those feelings. When faced with challenges and obstacles, I will not allow them to overcome me. I will look for the opportunities for growth in all circumstances.**

    _____ (initial)

- **I hereby declare that I am worth the time and effort that it will take to achieve the goals that I have set for myself.**

    _____ (initial)

- **I realize that my transformation will not occur immediately. Therefore, I will exercise patience with myself. I will not view my set-**

backs as failures, but as learning experiences designed to make me stronger and wiser.

_____ (initial)

- **I will assume the total responsibility for my thoughts, decisions, words, and actions, and will not relinquish this control to anyone.**

_____ (initial)

- **It is my belief that God has placed me here for a definite reason, and it is His desire that I fulfill that purpose for the good of mankind and myself.**

____ (initial)

I promise myself to abide by the terms of this contract and agree that I am bound by it until I achieve my goal.

_____

Your signature and date

Then I realized that it is good and proper for a man to eat and drink, and to find satisfaction in his toilsome labor under the sun during the few days of life God has given him-for this is his lot. Moreover, when God gives any man wealth and possessions, and enables him to enjoy them, to accept his lot and be happy in his work—this is a gift of God. He seldom reflects on the days of his life, because God keeps him occupied with gladness of heart.

(Ecclesiastes 5:18-20NIV)

REFERENCES

Robert N. Barger, Ph.D. University of Notre Dame, 2000. "A summary of Lawrence Kohlberg's Stages of Moral Development."

Albert Ellis, Ph.D., 1994, "Reason and Emotion in Psychotherapy Revised", Secaucus, NJ: Birch Lane.

Albert Ellis, Ph.D., 1996. "Better, Deeper, and More Enduring Brief Therapy: The Rational Emotive Behavior Therapy Approach." New York: Brunner/ Mazel

Albert Ellis, Ph.D. Catherine MacLaren, MSW, 1998. Rational Emotive Behavior Therapy, *A Therapist Guide Vol.II,* San Luis Obispo, CA Impact Publishing Inc.

William J. Federer, 1994. America's God and Country Encyclopedia of Quotations. Fame Publishing, Inc. Coppell, Texas 75019

Viktor E. Frankl, Ph.D. 1984, Man's Search For Meaning, Touchstone Books, Simon and Schuster Publishing Inc, New York, New York 10020

International Bible Society, 1984. New International Version Bible, International Bible Society, Colorado Springs, CO 80921-3696

Arnold A. Lazarus, Ph.D., Clifford N. Lazarus, Ph.D., 1997. The 60 Second Shrink, Barnes and Noble 1999, New York, New York

W. Matthys, J.M.Cuperus, & H.van Engeland, 1999. "Deficient Social Problems-Solving in Boys with ODD/CD, with ADHD, and with Both Disorders." *Journal of the American Academy of Child and Adolescent Psychiatry,* 38, pg 311-321.

Daniel Burton-Rose, Dan Pens, Paul Wright (Eds.): The Celling of America: *An Inside Look at the U.S.*

Prison Industry. Common Courage Press; Reprint edition (February 1998)

Gary Smalley, 1996. <u>Making Love Last Forever</u>, Word Publishing Group, Thomas Nelson Publishing, 1996, Nashville, TN 37214

ABOUT THE AUTHOR

Keith E. Jackson, is a former NFL football player who is currently employed as a correctional counselor for the San Diego County Sheriff's Department. He provides psycho-educational programs for the inmate population. Prior to his current position, he was a juvenile probation officer for twenty years. During his twenty years as a probation officer, Mr. Jackson was a trainer of trainers in the area of gang and cultural awareness. He also was an adjunct instructor, in the field of juvenile justice, at Southwestern College, in Chula Vista, CA. Keith obtained his B.A. degree in psychology from the University of Arizona, and his Master's Degree in counseling psychology from Southern California Bible College and Seminary. In addition, he has authored two books, Parents, Teach Your Kids to R.A.P. and Generation XIII, (A Guide to Understanding Street Gangs)

www.olcoutreach.org